VALERIE PATTERSON

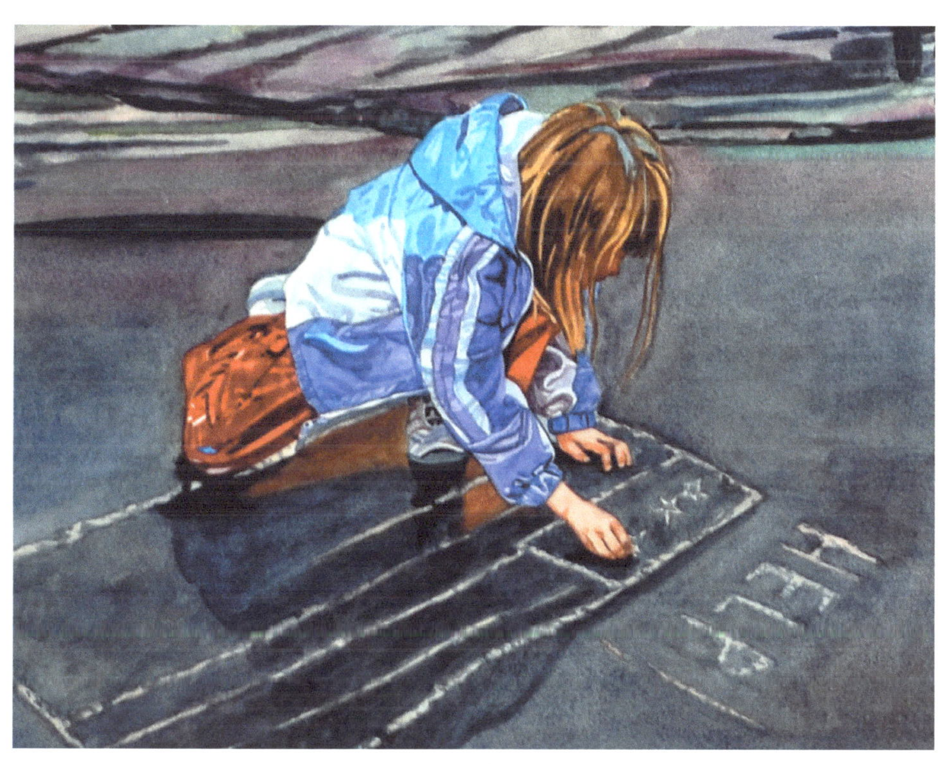

ART
TO START
THE
CONVERSATION

Discover more Valerie Patterson Art:

valeriepatterson.com

Designed and published by

ABCarlson Publishing, Keene, NH

ISBN: 978-0-9962883-3-0

Library of Congress Control Number: 2022942348

Contents

Introduction

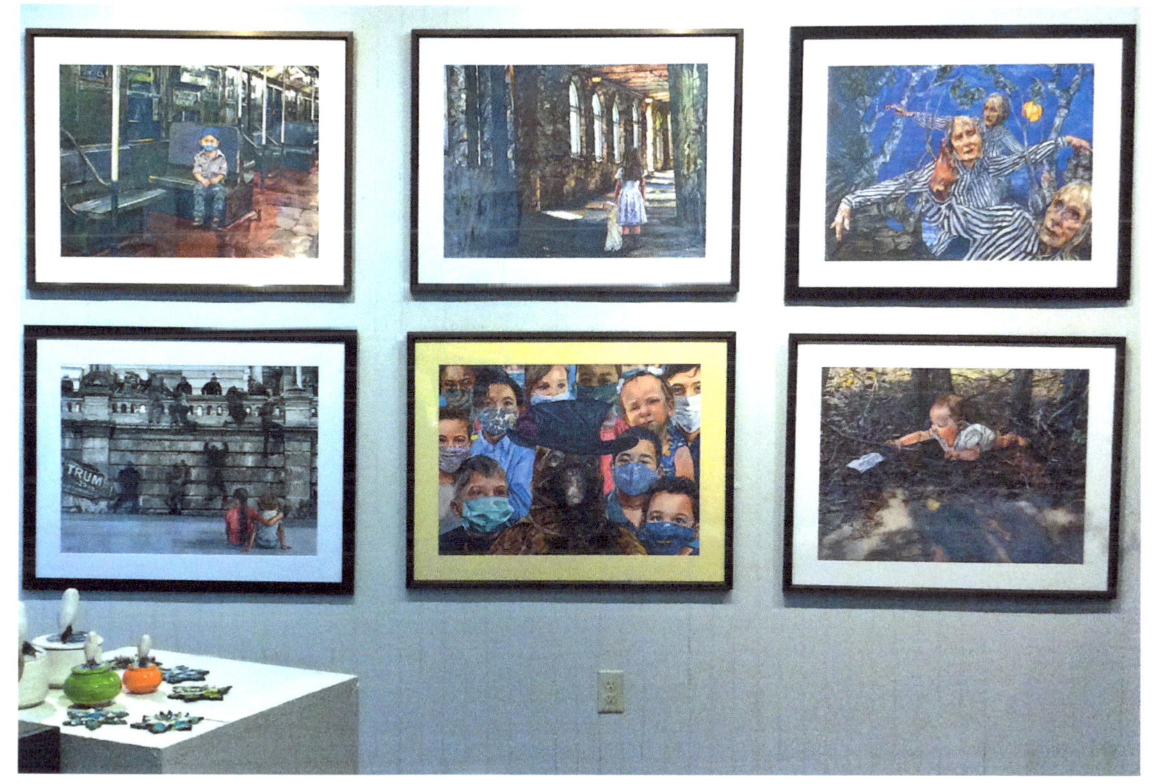

Valerie Patterson's watercolor paintings first came to my attention when I selected her as the winner of the Manhattan Arts International Magazine Cover Art Award in 1999. Immediately, I was awestruck by the powerful visceral impact her art has on the viewer and how she raises awareness about imperative personal, social and political issues.

Over the years I have watched Valerie evolve into an internationally recognized leader in contemporary narrative realism. Her inimitable style and technical prowess as a watercolor painter are matched by her profound insight that resonates truth, knowledge and understanding of the human condition.

Valerie conveys intense emotion with a proficient attention to detail — from the handling of her subjects' facial and body expressions to their seamless engagement within their environments. She often layers images to suggest time lapses and fuses realism with surreal elements. The cinematic quality she achieves adds an enthralling depth, dimension, and movement to her visual stories.

With astonishing versatility, Valerie fearlessly probes a huge range of topics — from poignant situations with children and the elderly to controversial political figures and events — that would stymie most artists.

Every thought-provoking painting Valerie creates is an integral part of her "Art to Start the Conversation" portfolio. The message-driven works of art often strike a nerve and take us outside our comfort zones. She wakes us up from our self-absorbed complacency and state of denial. We are compelled to examine vital questions about our beliefs, convictions, and social responsibilities.

Valerie ignites the flame for our capacity to feel and express empathy and compassion. Her art encourages "conversation" with others as we share our interpretations of her narrative themes, especially with those who may not share our views. This important dialogue fosters the potential for our crucial growth for tolerance, acceptance, and unity. In her hands art serves as a catalyst for creating positive transformation.

— Renee Phillips
Director/Curator, Manhattan Arts International, NYC, NY

Artist's Statement

Images have power. As an artist, I am always mindful of this and believe it important to create images which transcend the mere decorative, to illustrate thoughts and ideas. My work represents an extensive exploration of facets of the human condition and experience. I am fascinated by the psychology in every gesture and the universal within the personal. Being a spiritual humanitarian, my work often gives voice to social and political subjects — urging viewers to think and feel. I hope my paintings will provoke conversation. Only when we recognize and face difficult issues will we consider the possibility of creating change.

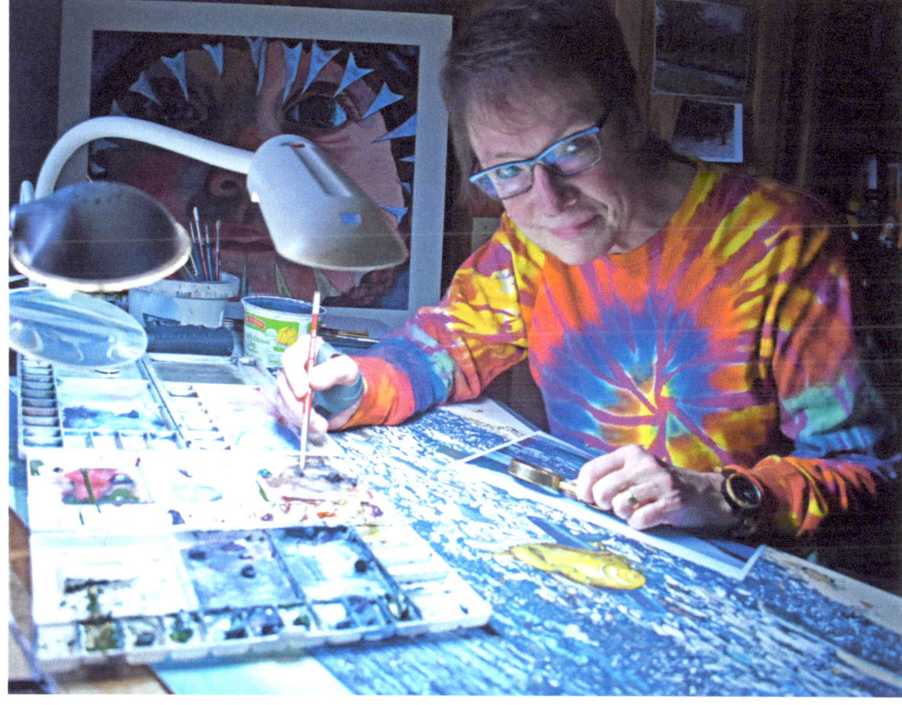

Throughout my paintings, children and the elderly represent innocence and vulnerability, black and white backgrounds are highlighted with figures in color symbolizing past and present as well as life and death, ghosts appear between layers of reality, and realistic and fantastic images are unexpectedly placed together to create surreal storyscapes.

I work in a hyper-realistic style so as to present flawless illusions. When I began painting in college, I painted realistic miniatures in oil. As my life circumstances changed, I decided to try watercolor due to its almost immediate drying time, which allowed me to carry my work with me wherever I went. I transferred my oil painting techniques into watercolor — glazing and layering color. The rebel in me appreciates, while vehemently disagreeing with, the fact that watercolor has often been considered a "lesser" medium.

ABOUT THIS BOOK

While considering the creation of this book, I find myself reluctant to include written commentary along with the paintings. A good work of art should be strong enough to stand on its own merits. I paint because, for me, communicating visually is a more pure, accurate and precise form of conveyance than the spoken or written word. I strongly believe that what YOU, the viewer, bring to a work of art, in terms of your life experiences, is just as significant and valid as any artist's intentions. Additionally, I often feel as though the ideas for my paintings come through me and not from me. Sometimes, I simply don't know where they come from. It is as if someone has whispered them in my ear. Nevertheless, I realize that as human beings we want to make a connection, to get to know and understand each other. Stories and back stories make us feel a part of something larger than ourselves. So, to that end, I present the following works and connected thoughts for your consideration.

In an attempt to organize the images contained in this book, I have divided them into four sections or chapters. Each is meant to set a tone or mood. Certainly, many of the paintings could comfortably exist in more than one of these categories.

It is my sincere hope that the paintings in this book resonate with pieces of your soul, instigate contemplation, and start some salient conversations…

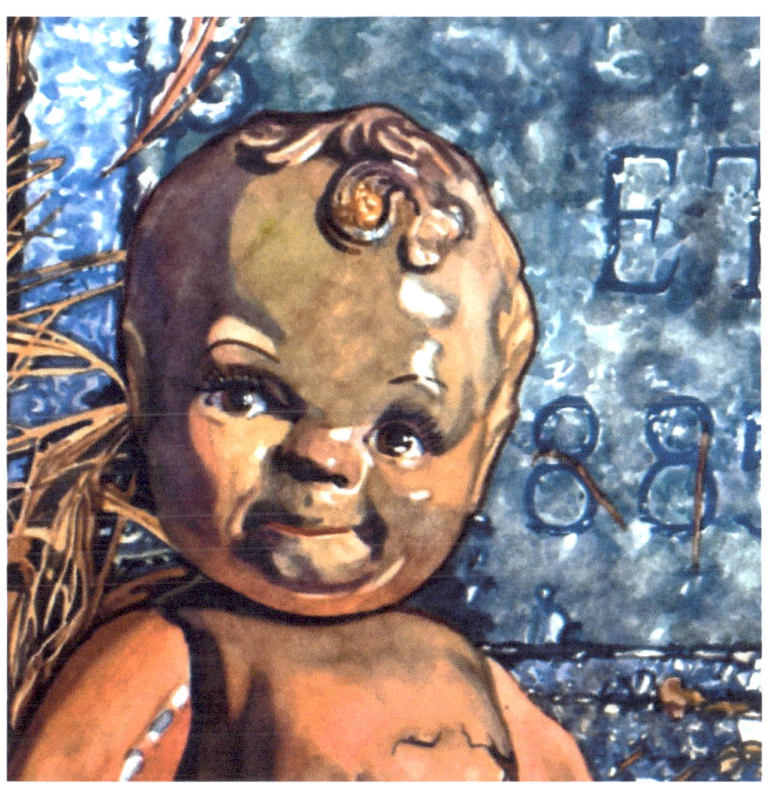

TIME

Our lives and experiences are ephemeral. Past, present and future, which mark our earthly existence on this plane, are no more than relative illusions. We are like holograms, Plato's shadows on the wall of the cave. Yet, the passing of time has deep meaning for us; we are educated within its evanescent constructs.

The doll that I utilized in this painting was given to me by a friend that has since passed. It belonged to her mother and then her younger sister, before becoming part of her inheritance. My guess is that it dates from the 1930s. The toy's name is Kathleen Marie, after the middle names of her first two owners. Kathleen Marie has appeared in several of my paintings representing the past, history, innocence and childhood. This painting began merely because I enjoyed the juxtaposition and emotional weight of the grave stone (photographed at a local cemetery) and the doll X 2. I consciously had no greater purpose for its creation — until attempting to title it. As odd as it may seem, I sometimes don't understand what a painting's purpose is until someone or something points it out to me. While contemplating a title, I came across the meaning of "grateful dead." Unbeknownst to me, it wasn't just a famous rock band! "Grateful dead" refers to folktale narratives concerning the spirit of a deceased person who bestows benefits on the one responsible for his burial.

This artwork begs numerous questions. Where did these dolls come from? Why are there two? Who do they belong to? Is Etta their mother, or...? What are the dolls doing there? Are they responsible for her burial? Does this represent a ceremony or funerary rites of sorts?

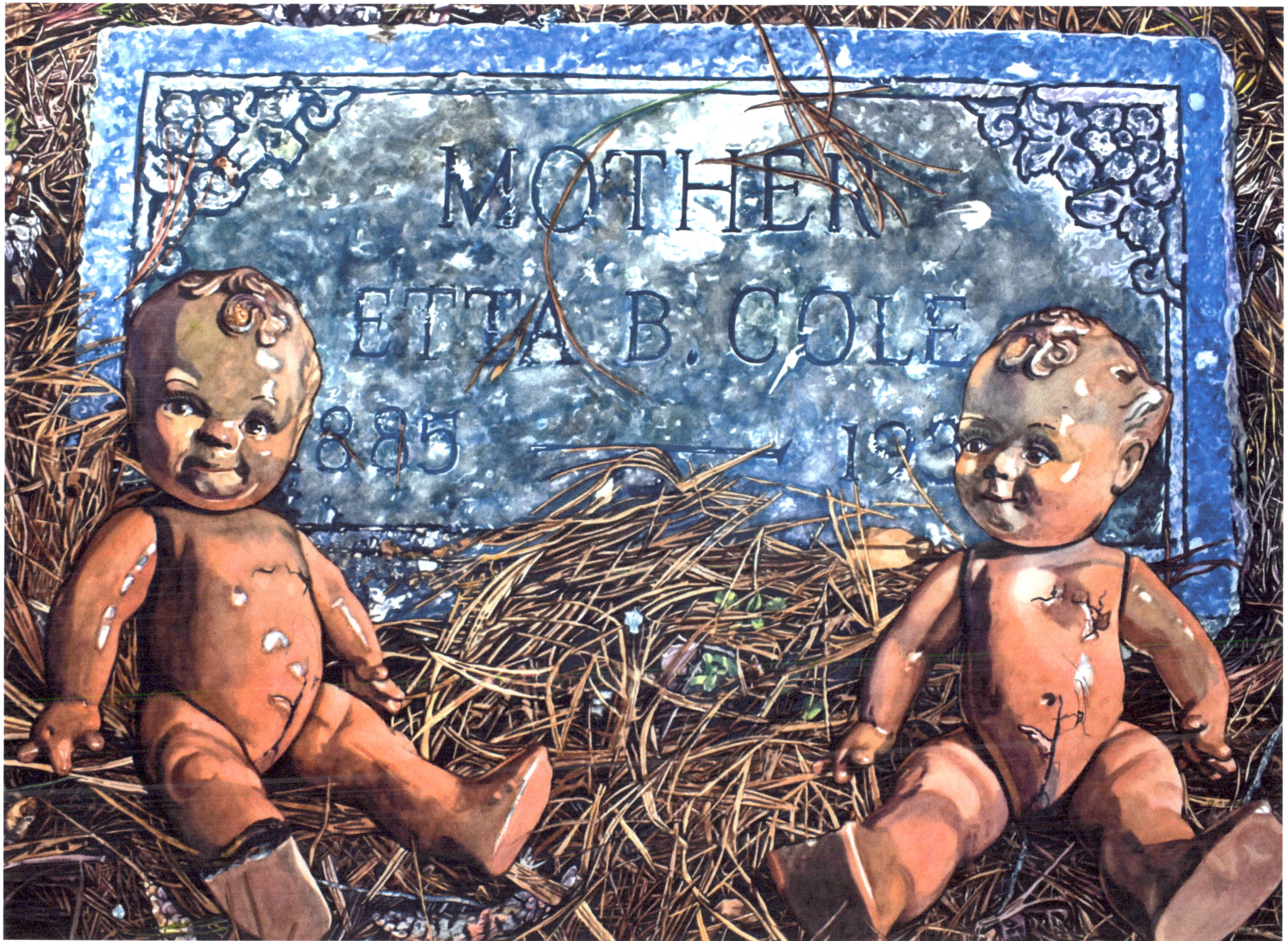

Our Grateful Dead   2021 (27" x 35")

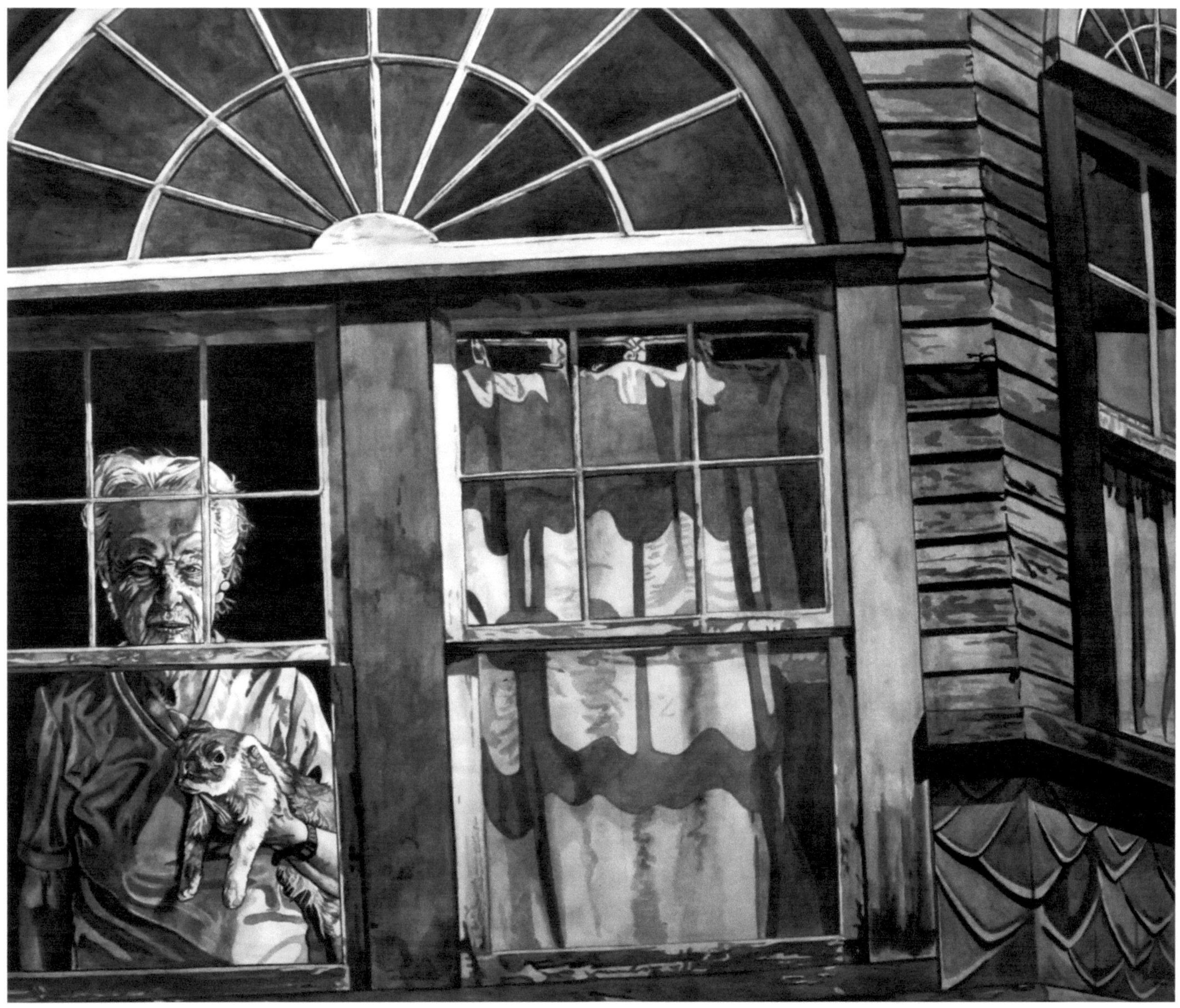

Expectations   2004 (31" x 36")

Aging isn't for the faint hearted, as the old adage goes. Not only does our physical body break down, we lose friends, family, jobs, memory, a sense of purpose, financial security, etc. Our worlds shrink and close in as everyday tasks become difficult. Scary stuff. However, there are upsides to old age as well. Self confidence may soar (I especially like this one!). We may experience less stress, and with it less anger. I was contemplating all of these things when I came across an old photograph of my maternal grandmother and her cat. I paired her with a building in Keene, NY, that I often drive by. I love the calm and contentment on her face. Her existence inside this painting, while limited to home, cat friend, and the views out her window, is a good enough one, I hope. As I age, this work continues to take on deeper meaning for me.

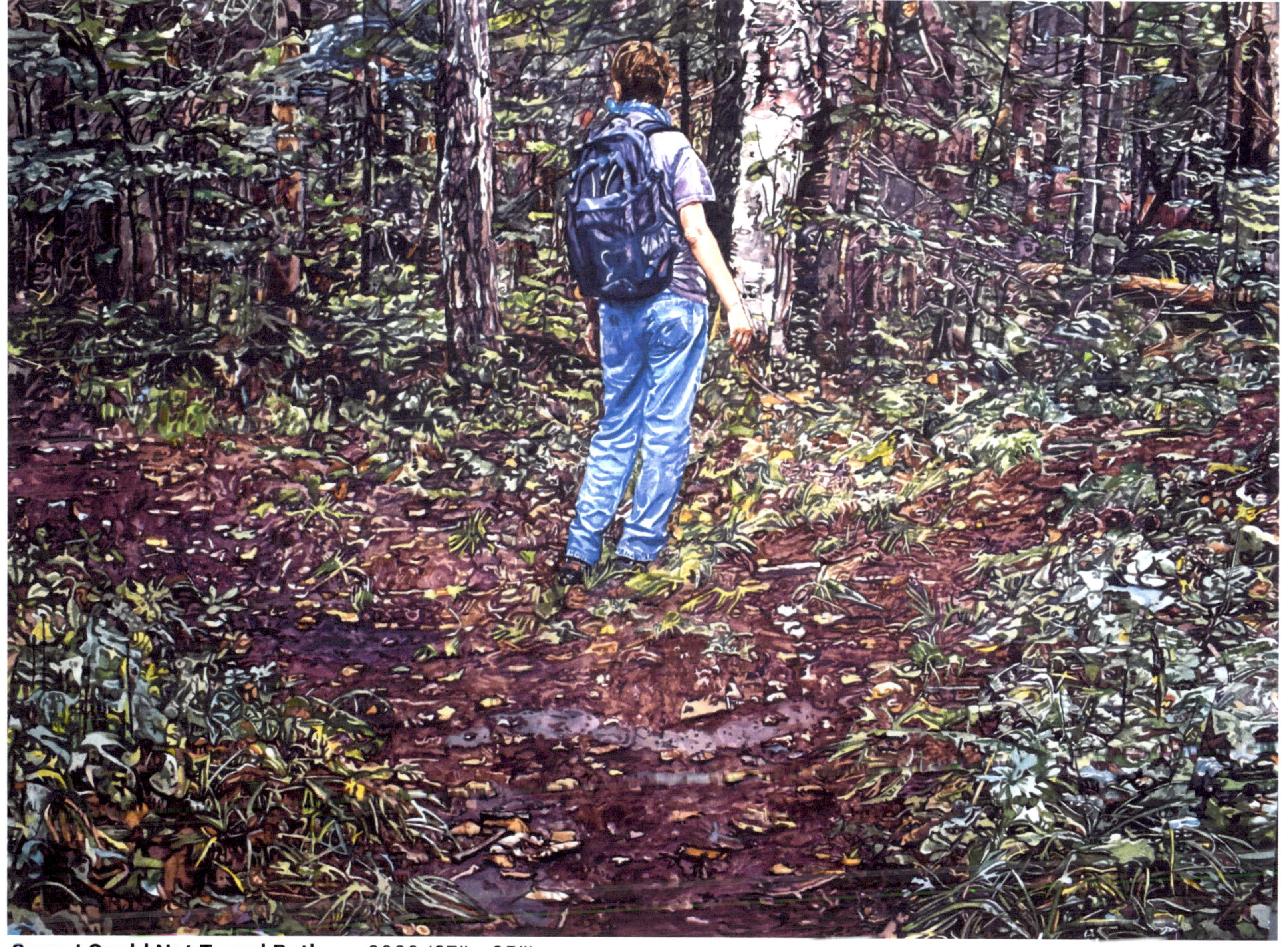

Sorry I Could Not Travel Both   2020 (27" x 35")

As you may well know, "sorry I could not travel both" is a line from the famous Robert Frost poem *The Road Not Taken*. This poem repeatedly whispers to my soul. When my spouse and I were hiking down a beautiful trail in the Adirondacks, and we came upon two paths diverged, I felt a strong urge to take some photos. This painting came about. Did she take the road less traveled? Did you?

I find painting wooded landscapes challenging because of the patience factor. While my painting style is always labor intensive, strangely, painting every leaf becomes tedious even for me. I was pleased when work on this one was complete.

I have a series of paintings entitled *Ghosts of Saranac Lake*. They incorporate the past with the present while highlighting Saranac Lake's unique history, from the 1880's to the 1950's, as a health resort/sanitarium for people suffering from TB.

This series began after I toured an abandoned "cure cottage." While in this grand, rambling, beautiful old building, I couldn't help but feel the presence of those who had cured there. People who, because of an illness that was often a death sentence, left family and friends to come to the Adirondacks in hopes of relief — looking for a cure facilitated by some fresh mountain air, exercise, good food and rest. When I view old photos of the people "taking the cure" on the local porches of former sanitariums and cure cottages, I imagine myself into them. I wonder how those people confronted their lives at that moment. Pain, fear, discomfort, and loneliness were undoubtedly present, and yet many TB patients survived and lived long lives. There are numerous patients' stories of hope, survival and happiness. Many patients survived to describe their time taking the cure in the Adirondacks as being the best time of their lives, due to the tight knit community, hope and friendship. Imagine a community of people who truly knew the value of one day…one hour…one minute…

Taking The Air depicts the James Memorial Staff building (from behind) on the former grounds of the Trudeau Sanitarium, as it appears today. Sadly, it is in a state of decay and is being utilized for storage. The Trudeau tuberculosis sanitarium was established by Dr. Edward Livingston Trudeau in Saranac Lake, NY, in 1884. This particular building, named after Dr. Walter B. James, Trudeau's successor, was a residence for patients who were also doctors. I integrated an amiable group of patients' ghosts enjoying a present-time stroll, in honor of those souls that managed to take pleasure in the small but important matters of life within an existence focused on illness.

For me, the creation of ghosts involves making two separate paintings simultaneously. I have to concentrate on one image at a time (in this case either the people OR the background) while being keenly aware of the second image so that I don't let one dominate more than I want it to. It is a balancing act.

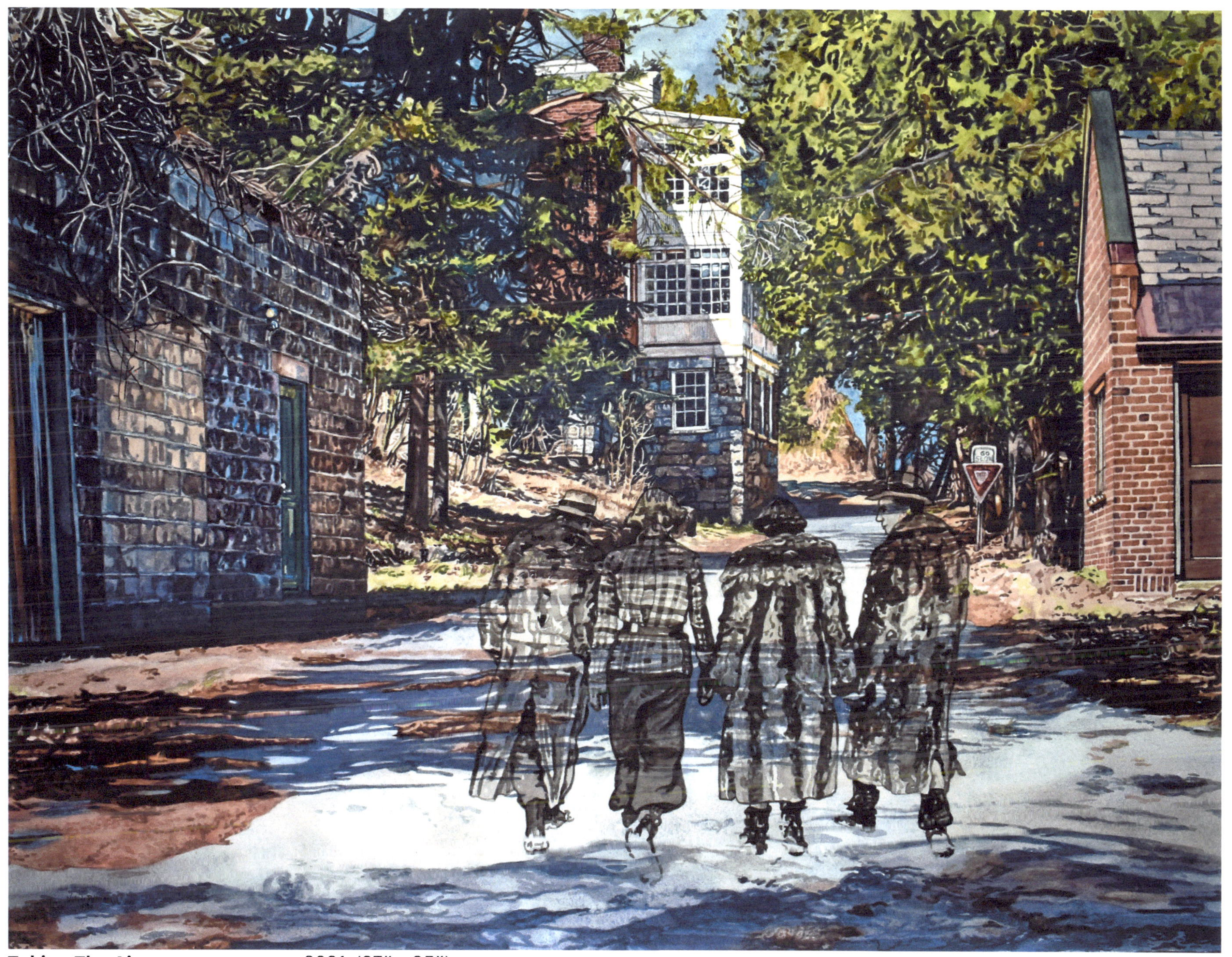

Taking The Air   2021 (27″ x 35″)

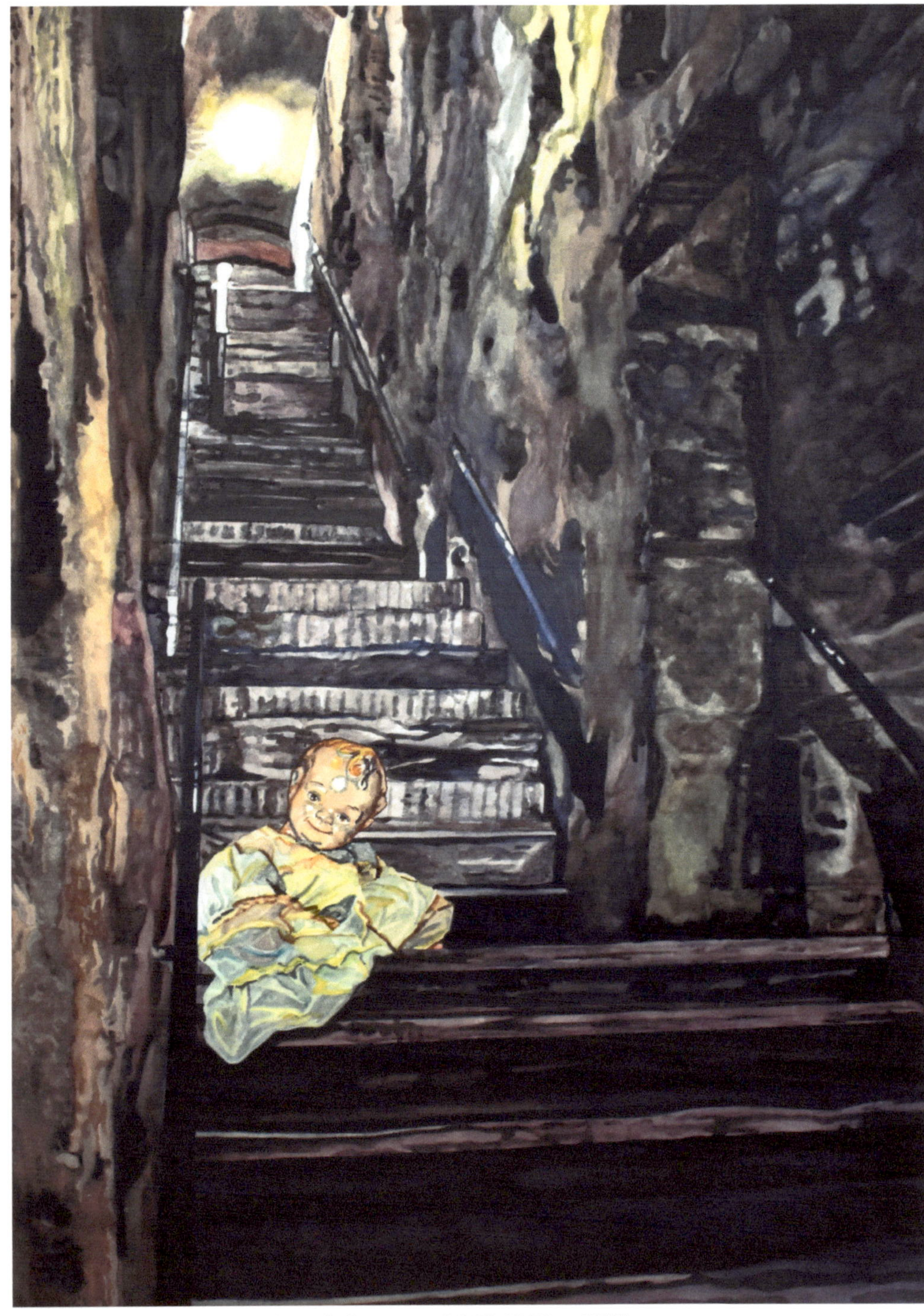

One Step Closer To The Light   2017 (35″ x 27″)

Childhood memories, while often delightful, may keep us in dark emotional places. Sometimes we need to take the time to "listen" to our personal past, in order to process memories and past events. The doll in this painting — on the steps, in the shadows — represents a forgotten piece of childhood. However, behind and above her, is light. The light is attainable, step by step, or processed memory by memory, as we change and evolve toward a more enlightened state.

Kathleen Marie (see *Our Grateful Dead*) made her painting debut in this work. I carefully posed her on the stairs leading to my studio, making certain that I photographed the doll and stairs from the same perspective as that in the separate photo of the ominous stairs. I put the images from the two photos together beginning with the pencil underdrawing, then painted the doll first, as that interested me most.

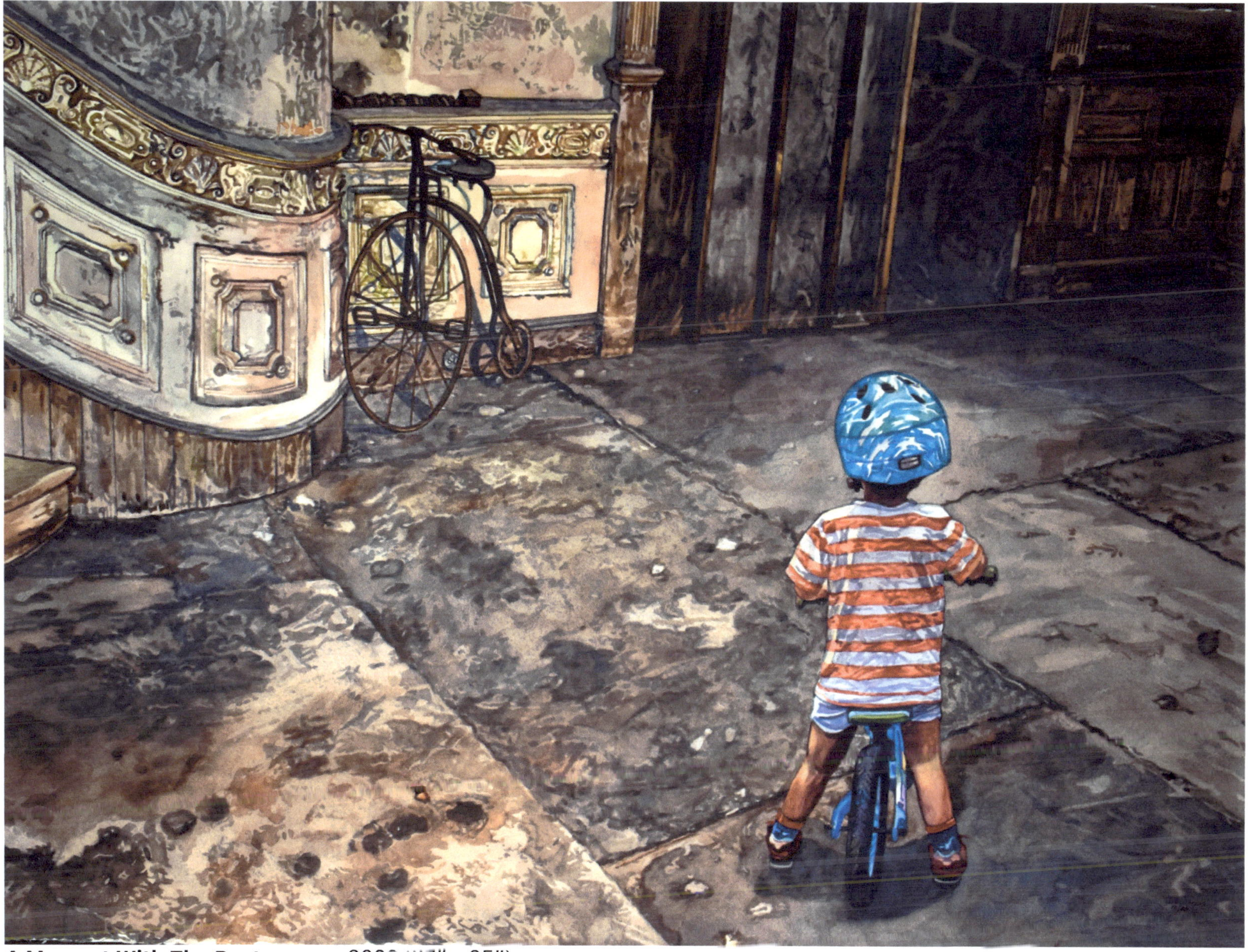

A Moment With The Past   2020 (27" x 35")

    While visiting Boldt Castle in the Thousand Islands region of New York, I happened upon this vintage penny-farthing (the first machine to be called a bicycle). I instantly envisioned a present-day child noticing and pondering this glorious piece of history for the first time, while bestride his own modern bicycle. This painting exemplifies a moment of psychological transtemporal travel. The little guy on the bike was liberated from a photo taken by a friend of mine.

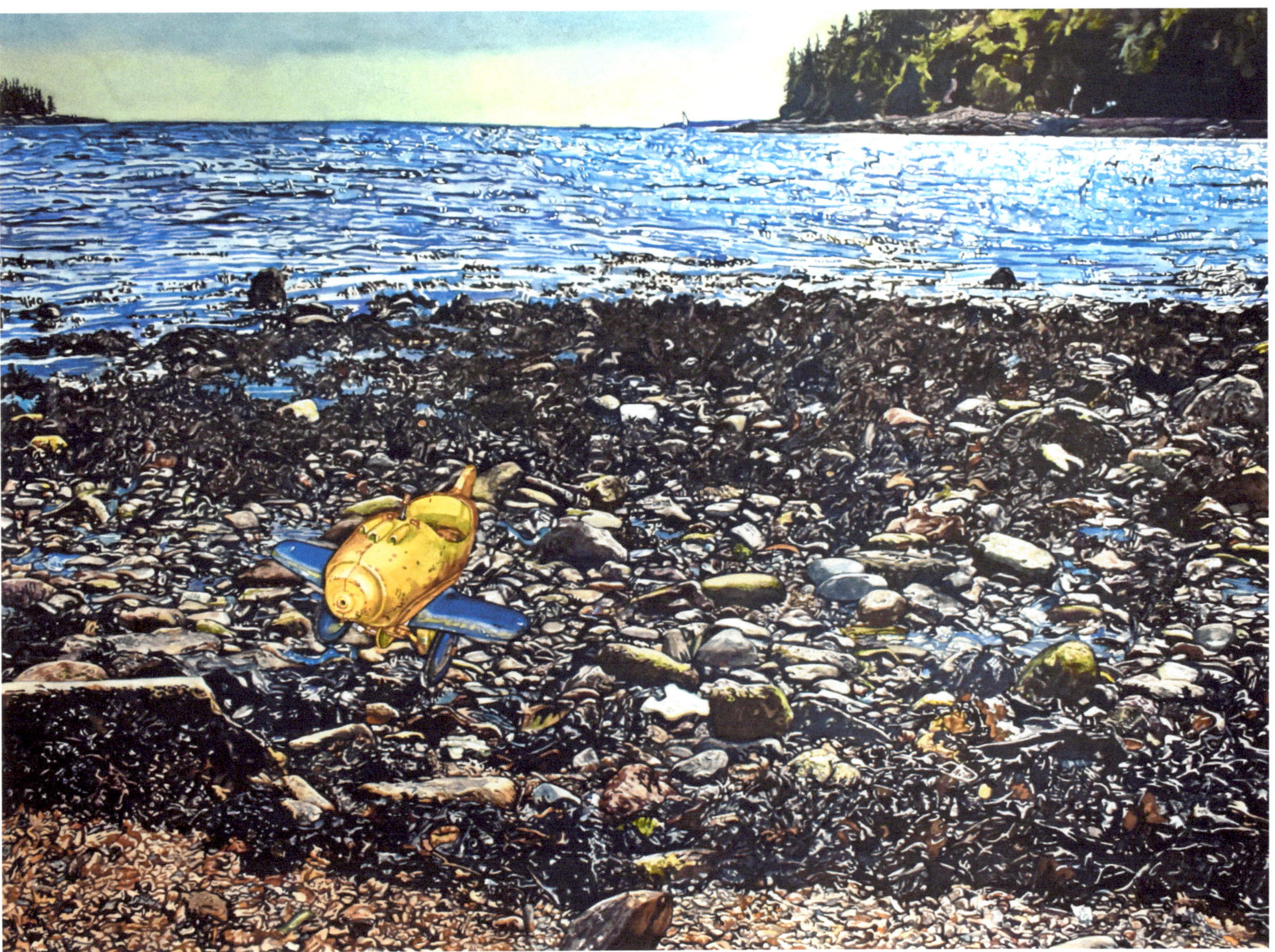

Newcomer   2022 (27" x 35")

To create this painting, I used a photo that I took along the shoreline while visiting Acadia National Park. The airplane originated from a photo I shot at the Seal Cove Auto Museum nearby, in Seal Cove, ME. I put the two images together because somehow, in conjunction, they transformed into a comforting paramnesia, or daydream, as follows: I am walking along a beautiful shoreline in Maine when I spot an object that immediately transports me to childhood; a childhood from this particular lifetime? I wonder, because this object — a child's ride-in pedal plane — was never something from my present life's childhood. And yet, there it is. A visceral response from my imagination. Childhood.

14

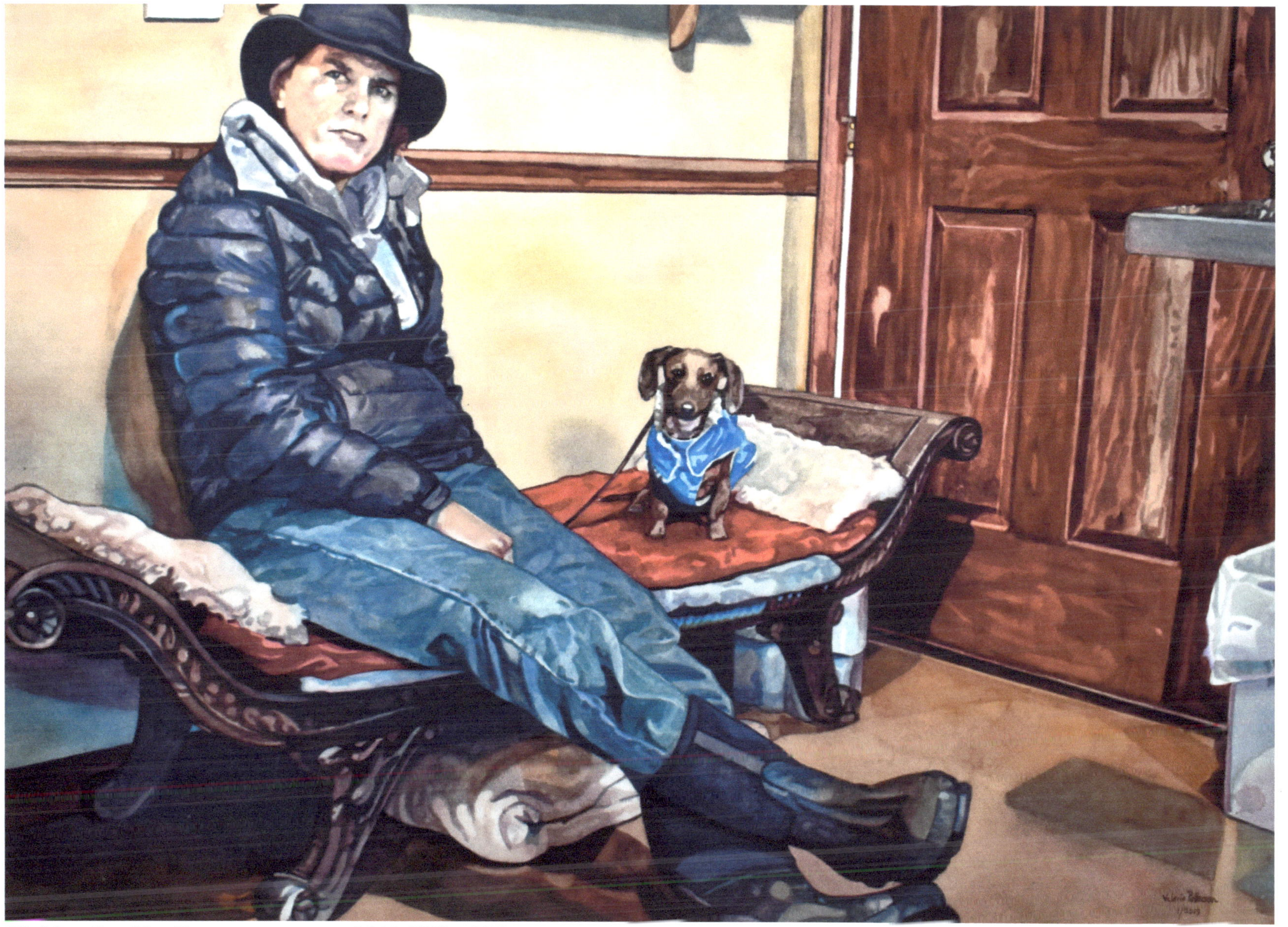

Waiting For The Vet 2019 (27" x 35")

   If you have a pet, you know the score: sitting, waiting, perhaps worrying alongside a dear one while you both eagerly anticipate the arrival of the trusted veterinarian. While being mindful of the situation and retaining a bit of patience, these are also unexpected, irreplaceable moments of attentiveness and love. I painted this image from a photo I took with my phone while waiting for the vet with my spouse and one of our pets. I love their matching expressions.

In 2017 I had the opportunity to visit the Eastern State Penitentiary in Philadelphia, PA. The Penitentiary, in operation from 1829 through 1971 and now touted as America's most historic prison, is open to visitors. It pioneered a system of separate incarceration emphasizing reform over punishment. One of its more notorious inmates was Al Capone. It is often purported to be a very haunted place; its most appealing feature as far as I am concerned. Although I believe in ghosts, as spirits that survive death and may be compelled to stick around this Earth for a variety of reasons, I truly didn't expect to encounter one here. And essentially, I didn't. Nevertheless, as soon as I walked into the first cell, my breathing constricted. I felt a sense of despair and an overpowering urge to flee. I believe I experienced a psychic imprint, a residual energy from the past. Imprints occur in specific locations where dramatic events have taken place. Sensitive people can feel this emotional energy for years afterwards.

I have created several paintings featuring cells from Eastern State Penitentiary. This painting presents a view down one of the more abandoned wings. It was closed off during my visit. Even so, I was able to take the photograph employed here. I added the ghost of an officer, perhaps a prison guard. I didn't want him to appear altogether present so I blurred him out a little with a damp paint brush. He is materializing.

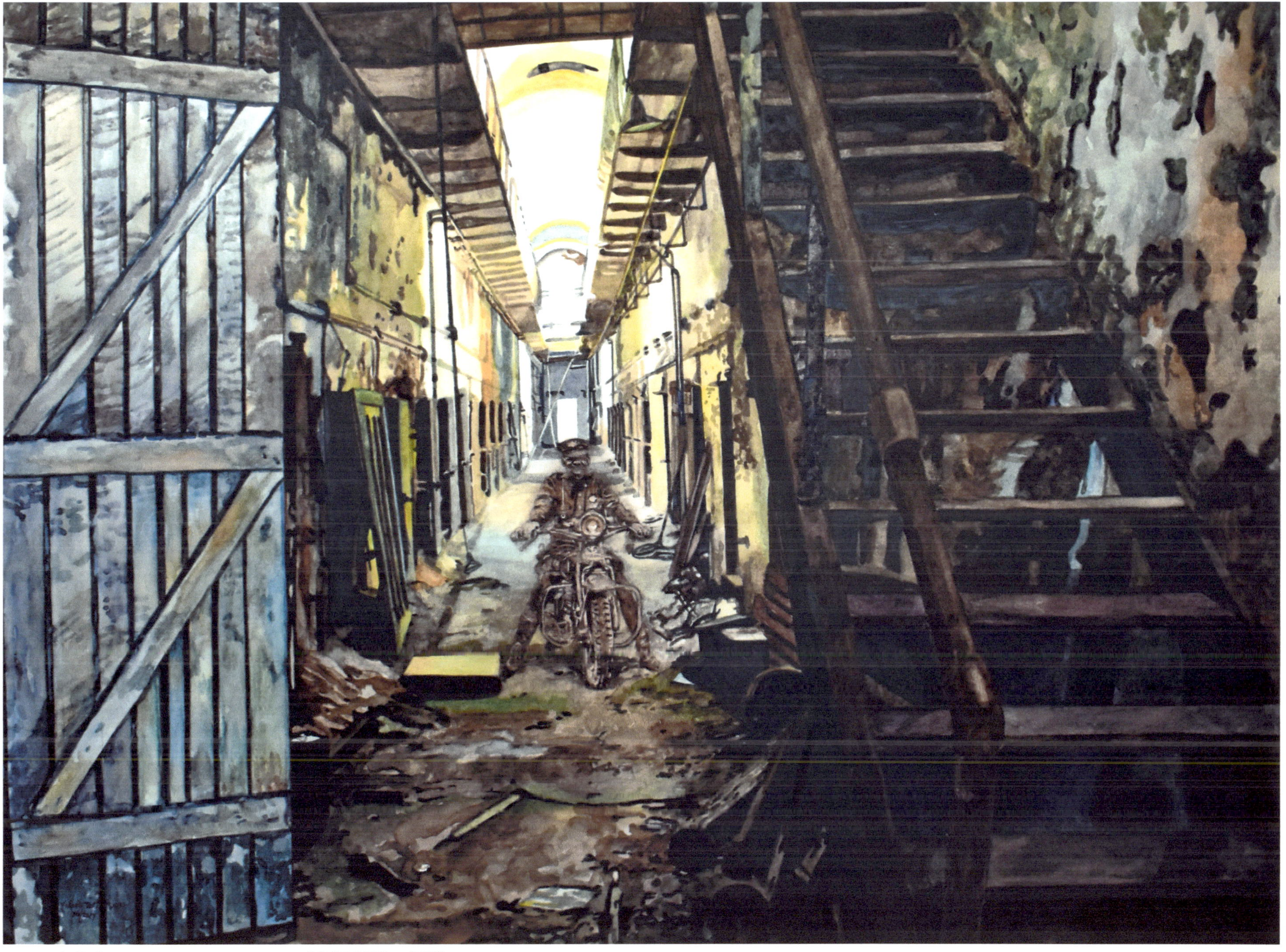

Materializing   2017 (27″ x 35″)

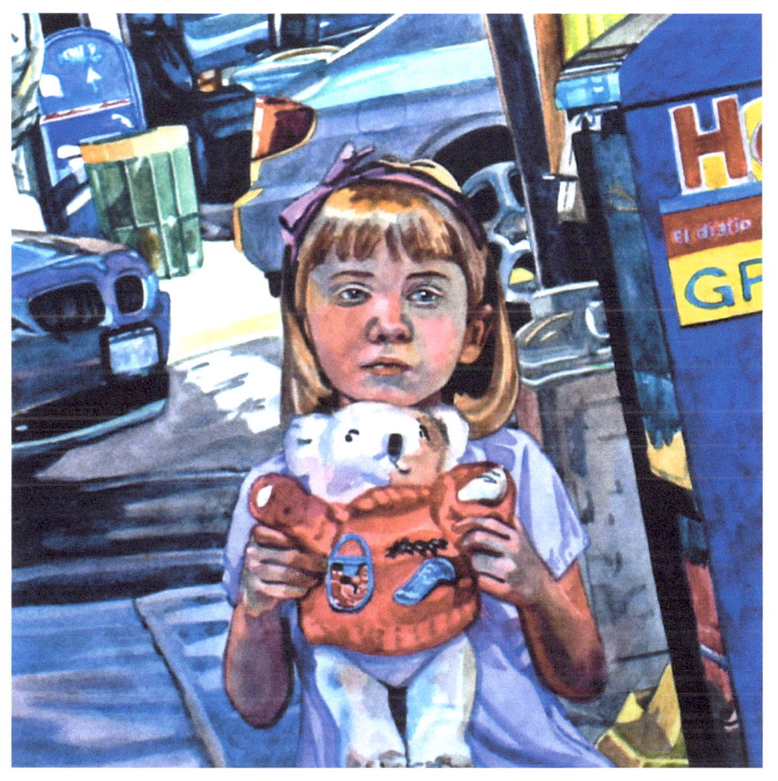

CHILDHOOD

Childhood could be viewed as a journey beginning in a state of innocence, traveling through extreme periods of research and education, and resulting in the growth and expansion of the soul and intellect. Many of our most vivid memories are created during this time and continue to influence us throughout our lives. Our childhood experiences make us who and what we are as adults. Childhood is paramount.

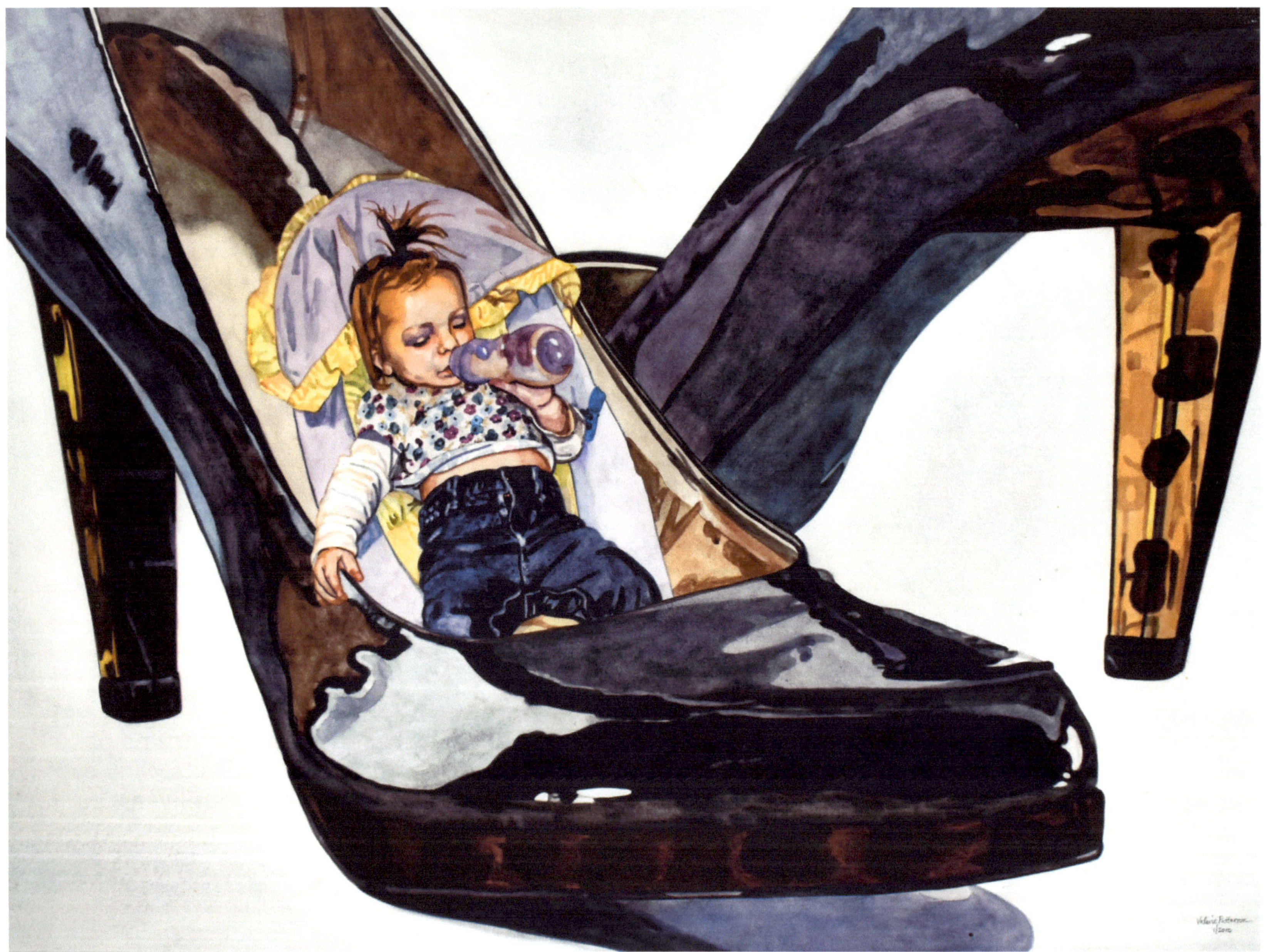

Good Fit?   2010 (27" x 35")

Our culture, in large part, can determine who we become on emotional and behavioral levels. Every culture has gender role expectations. Generally, females are expected to dress in feminine ways, to be supportive and amenable. But this isn't always a good fit. In truth, while one size may fit most, it doesn't fit all. In this painting I ask the question: are the cultural norms and expectations a good fit for this particular young girl? If not, does she possess the inner strength, self reliance and power to determine this and become her authentic self?

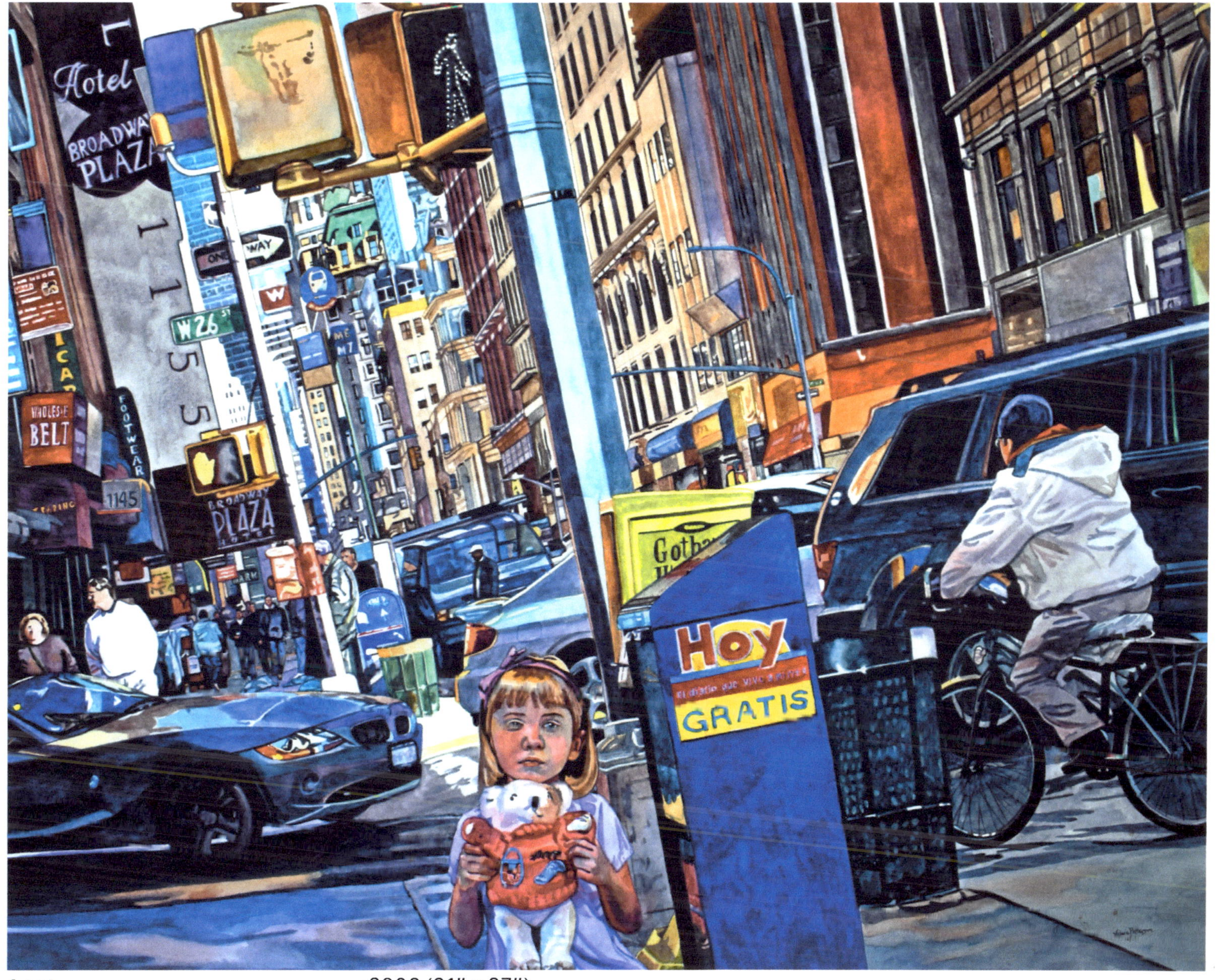

Lost   2006 (31" x 37")

Urban environs create much visual and emotional excitement, while also producing a terrifying sense that anything can happen at any moment. Filled with excessive stimulation, crowded NYC streets immediately overwhelm me. This painting came into existence with these sensibilities in mind. The little girl is lost and alone while being engulfed by the cityscape. *Lost* symbolizes a literal and spiritual searching for home and a sense of belonging, survival and inner peace.

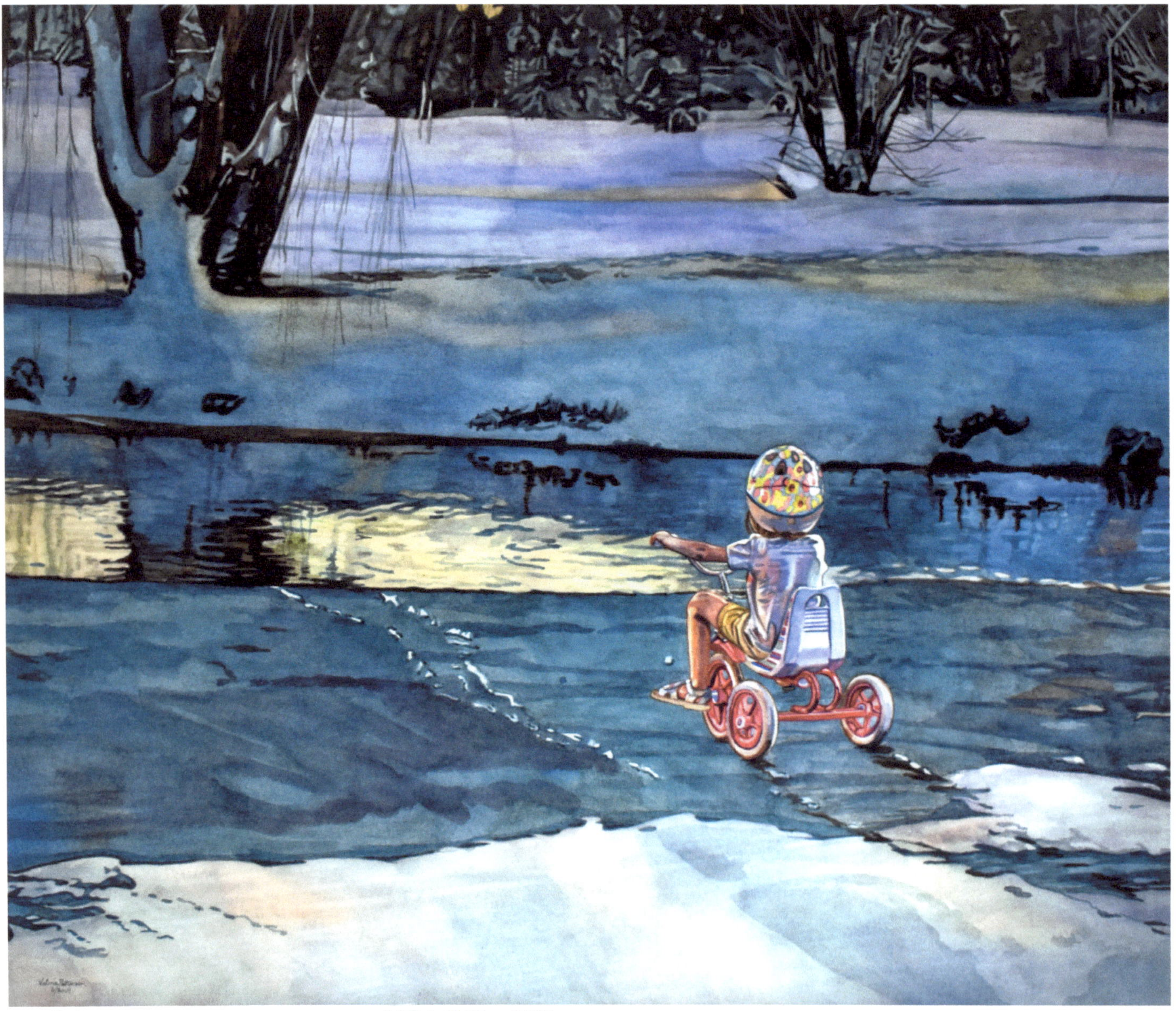

Twilight   2004 (31" x 35")

For me, this painting represents the beginning of a searching and learning cycle. The young child has begun her journey to self. She travels through space and time on her trike, perceiving the beauty in the waning twilight accompanied by the bitterness and potential danger of the ice, snow and open water. It's a silent, mysterious and significant moment of discovery.

I frequently come up with painting ideas by covering my studio floor with my photos. I study them and see which ones work together in some way or produce strong emotions or an engaging situation. *Twilight* came into being this way.

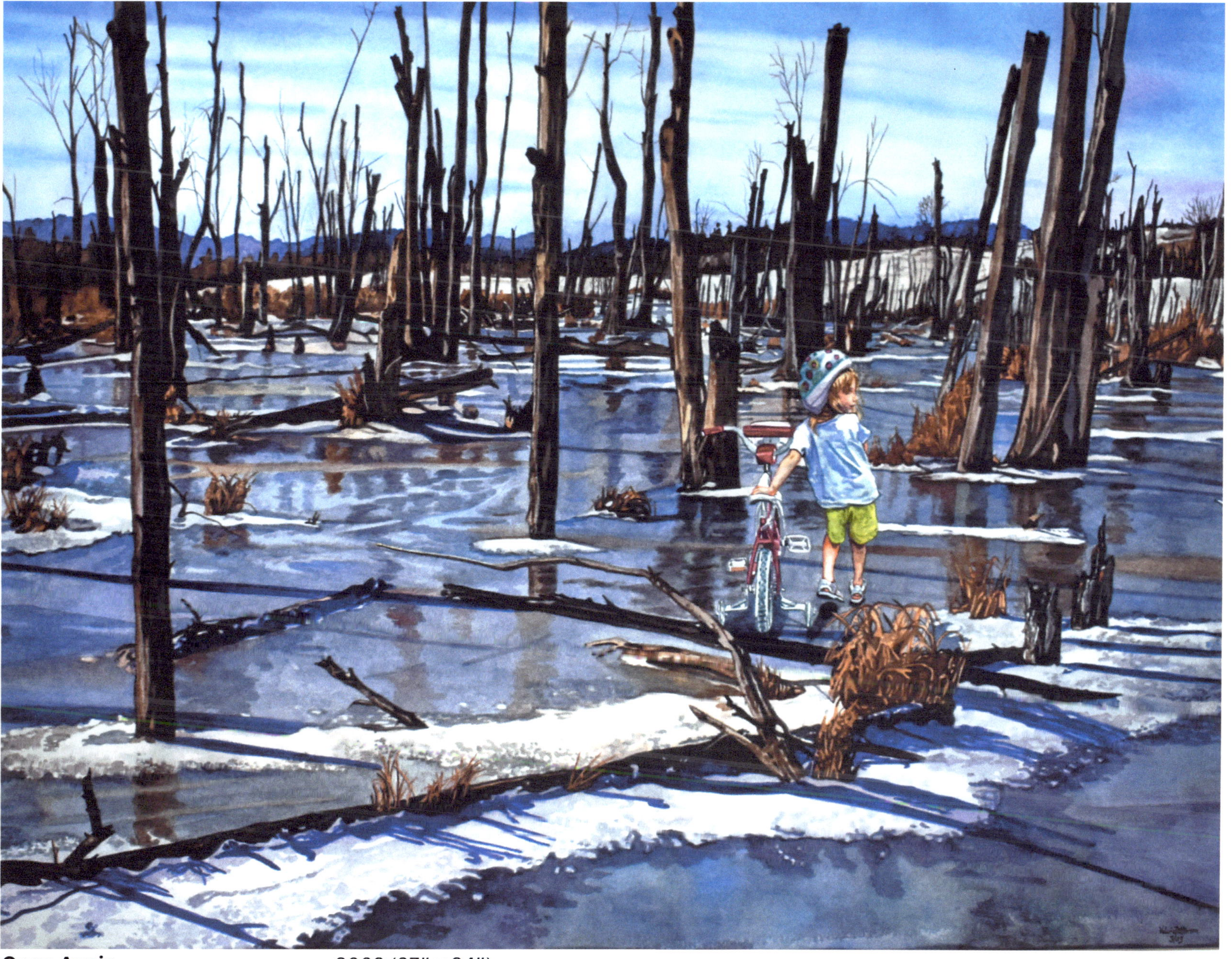

Once Again   2003 (27" x 34")

Despite her youth, the young girl experiences a difficult situation or challenging period (symbolized by an isolated, ice covered forest floor) once again — of what sort? Only she knows. Notwithstanding, the sun shines as she gazes off to the side, perhaps to a more optimistic future. She has a good deal of life ahead of her. This was another painting idea which came together from photos strewn about my studio floor.

In early 2020, before Covid closed down the world, I spent a few days at Disney's Magic Kingdom Theme Park in Orlando, Florida. In truth, it wasn't one of my bucket list destinations and my expectations weren't particularly high. But I am pleased to report that it transported me to a kind of childhood wonderment and revived some warm, long-lost memories and emotions. While waiting around near the bronze sculpture of Disney and Minnie Mouse, I captured some photographs (later used to create this painting) of this young girl enjoying what I considered a magical, enchanted, moment. It wasn't until later — when an acquaintance remarked how Disney had ruined her life by creating popular female characters as weak, domestic, damsels in distress — that I rethought this painting.

Certainly Disney films have reflected and intensified the society and culture of the times in which they were created. Original Disney characters such as Snow White and Cinderella relied on men for their happiness and well being. This has impacted girls and women in many negative ways by suggesting that a girl's most valuable asset was/is her physical appearance, that she should be submissive and expect to be rescued by a man, and believe in love at first sight. Fortunately, culture and Disney have shifted somewhat over time. More female Disney characters (Mulan, Merida, Elsa) are being portrayed as independent, rebellious, free spirited and strong willed.

There is almost always more to a work of art than first meets the eye.

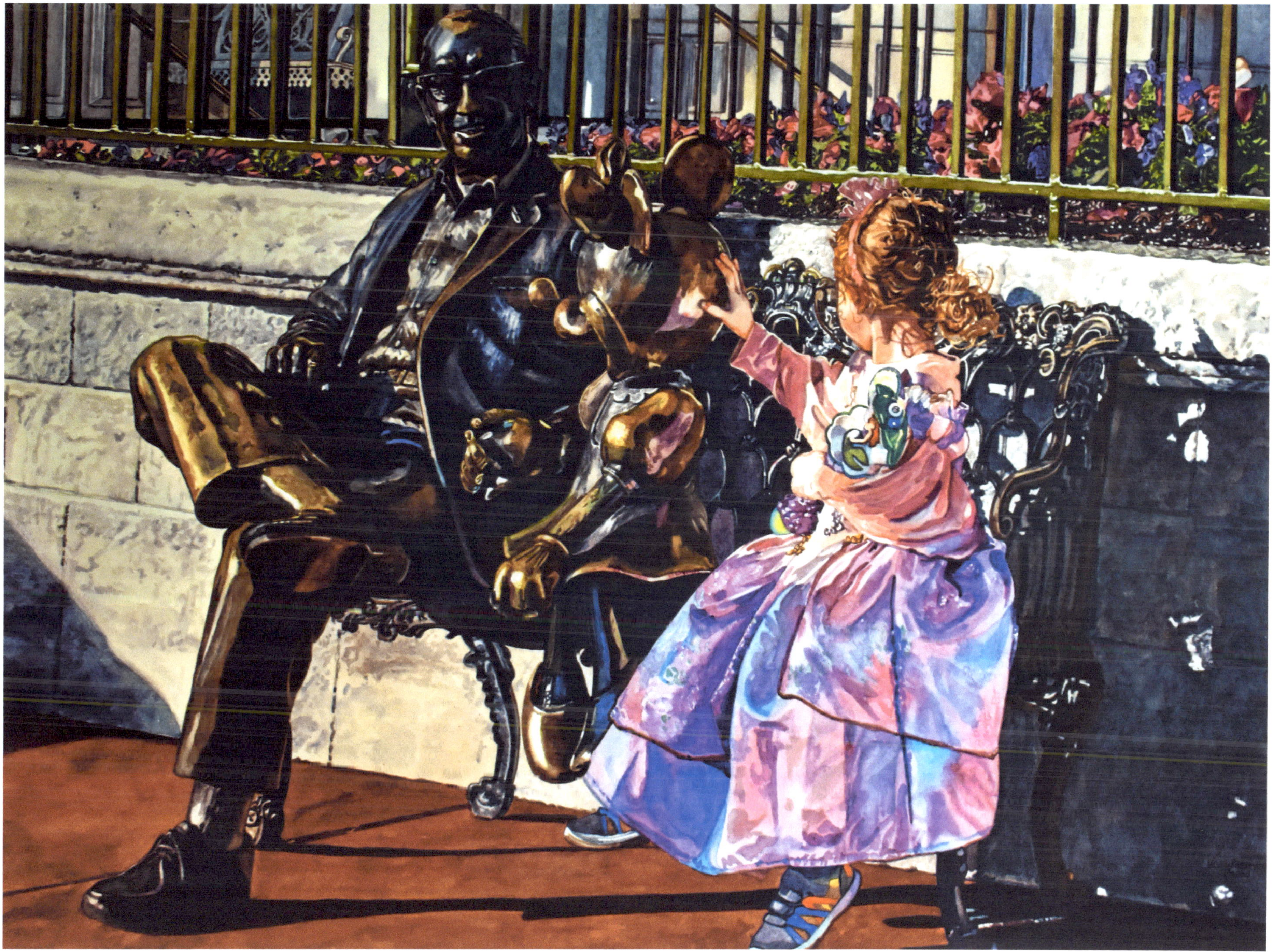

Enchantment   2019 (27" x 35")

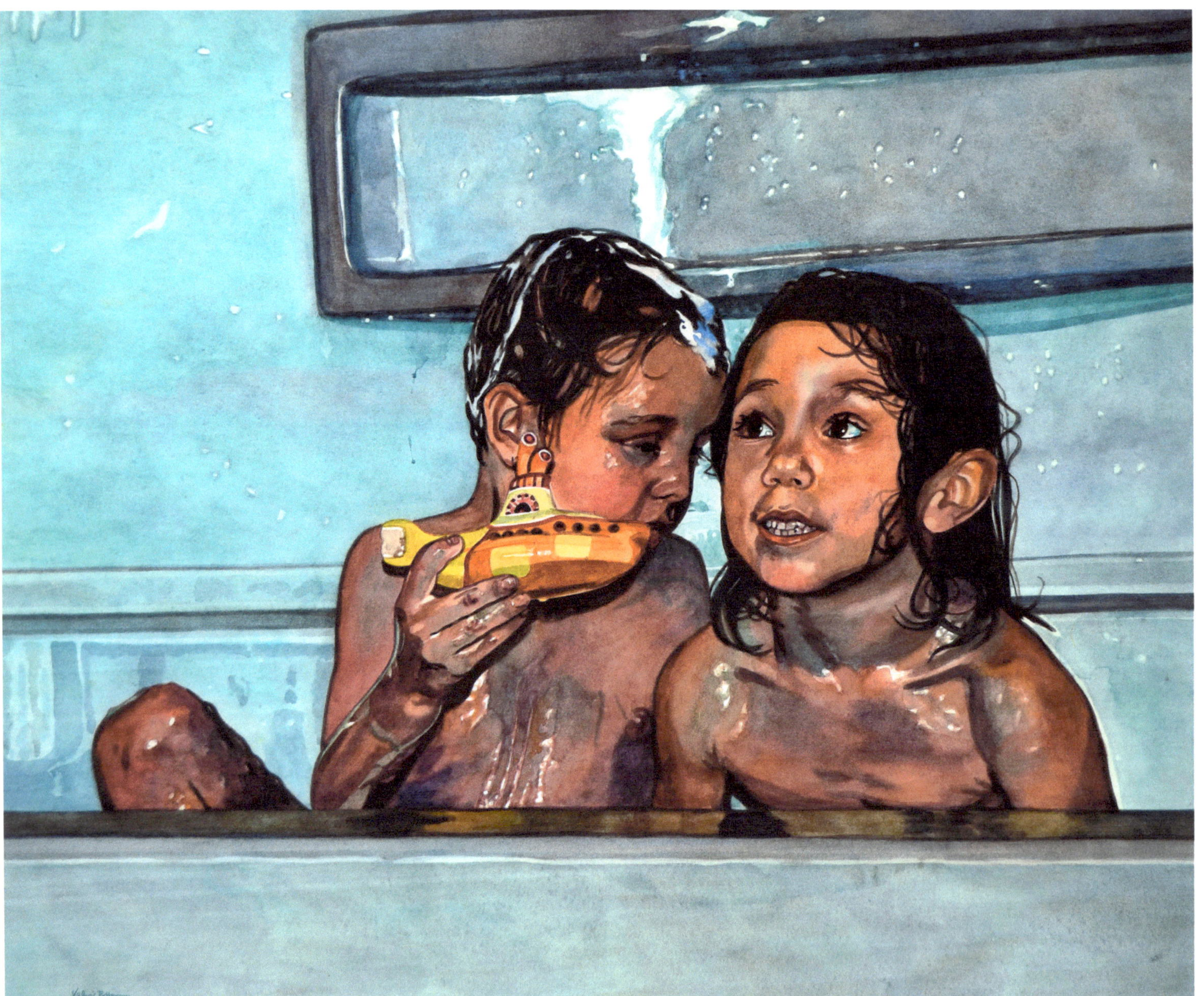

The Secret   2007 (31" x 36")

For awhile these two jaunty youngsters spent some time in my life. Fortunately for me, they never minded being photographed doing whatever they were doing. That is the best: being able to "capture" people "off guard" — being themselves. Often, as was the case here, I discover that I have recorded a moment of significance. Here these siblings share something top secret. What is its importance, its gravity? What are its implications? Only they will ever know. The yellow submarine (a toy of mine) is a nod to my favorite Rock band. Can you guess?

26

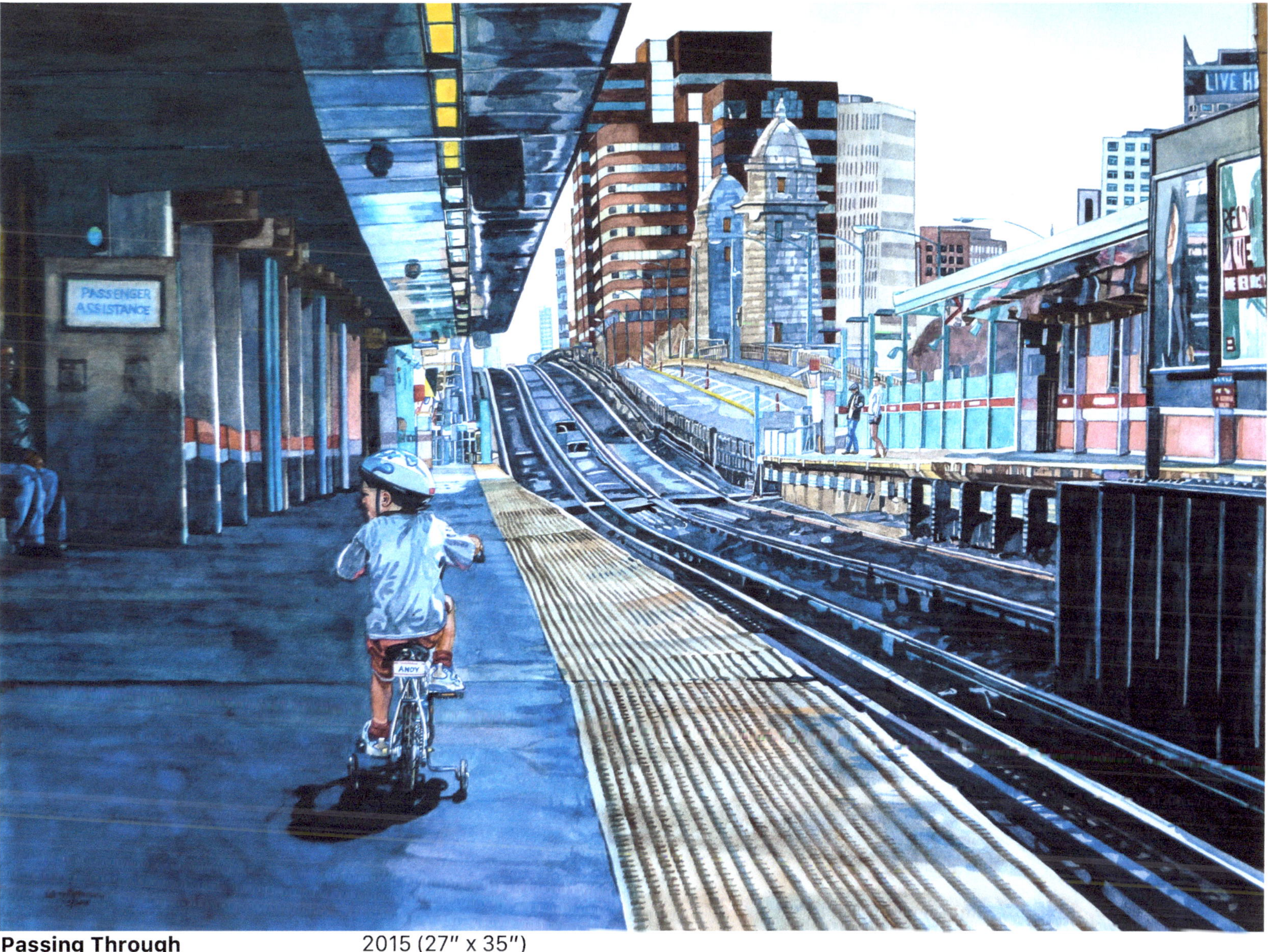

Passing Through   2015 (27" x 35")

Over several weeks, I spent some time at this Boston subway station while in the city for family medical reasons. This stop is next to Mass General. I was first visually struck by all of the "paths" created by the tracks, road and sidewalk. I was also impressed by the continually occurring, transient bits of life in this place. On the face of it, *Passing Through* depicts a young boy's journey through Boston's Charles Street/MGH MBTA station on his bicycle. But supposing the train tracks are a metaphor for moving through life/time. The boy and his bicycle are aligned with the path of the tracks. They travel side by side, forward in one inevitable line as he leaves the past behind. Will he continue along this way or suddenly veer from this deliberate path?

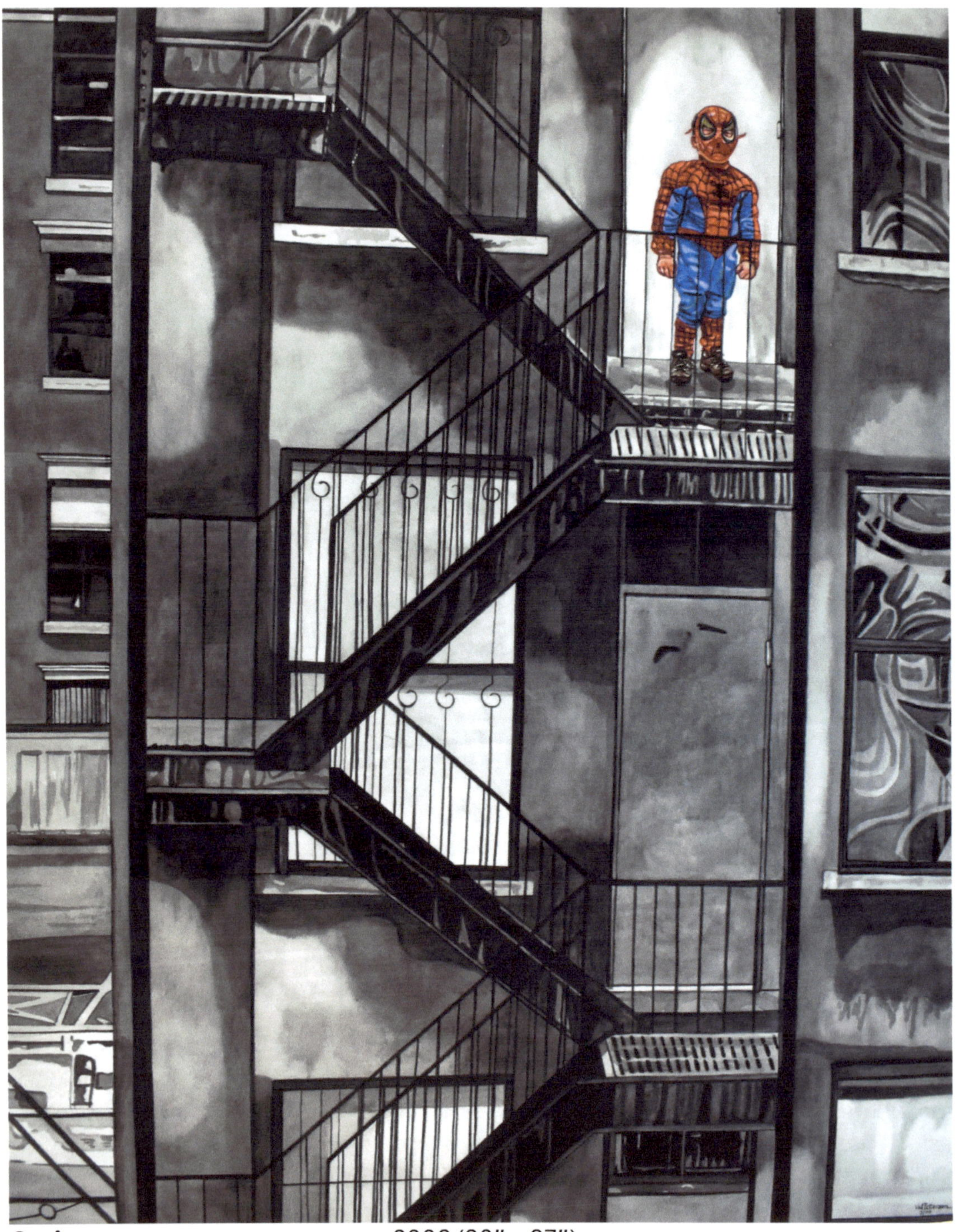

Savior · 2006 (30" x 37")

Sadly, we live in a time of hate, extreme polarization and hostility. How lovely it would be to have a real superhero in this dimension, to aid us and rescue us from peril and annihilation: a Being to inspire and be who and what we are not. Of course, our super hero must be a child: a conveyor of the legacy of the past and a symbol of future potential, a beacon of light amidst the darkness.

The little guy in this work was the son of a friend of mine. How fortunate I was to be able to photograph him proudly sporting his Spider-Man Halloween costume. Needless to say, I later painted him into an urban landscape where we can forever benefit from his special abilities.

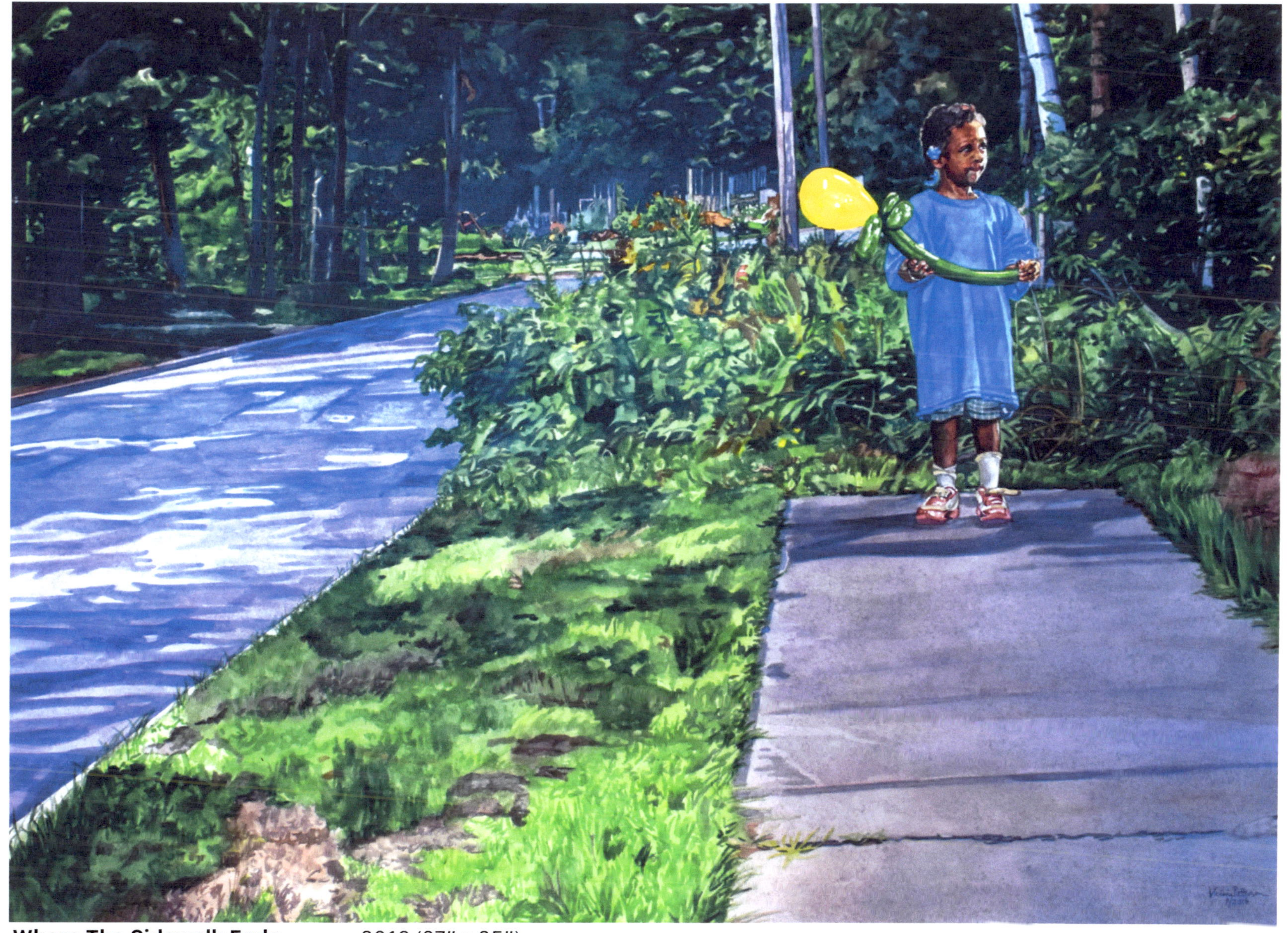

Where The Sidewalk Ends   2016 (27" x 35")

This sidewalk truly does end at this very place in Saranac Lake, NY. It is down a street where I enjoy taking walks. This painting is a nod to the Shel Silverstein poem of the same name. Silverstein's poem proposes that where the sidewalk ends is a magical place of childhood and innocence. This is also the contention in my painting. However, because the young girl is African American, issues of race inevitably come into play, potentially creating a myriad of scenarios. The flower balloons represent receptivity and wonder. The girl stares off to the side. What or whom does she see? Is she being acknowledged? You choose the storyline.

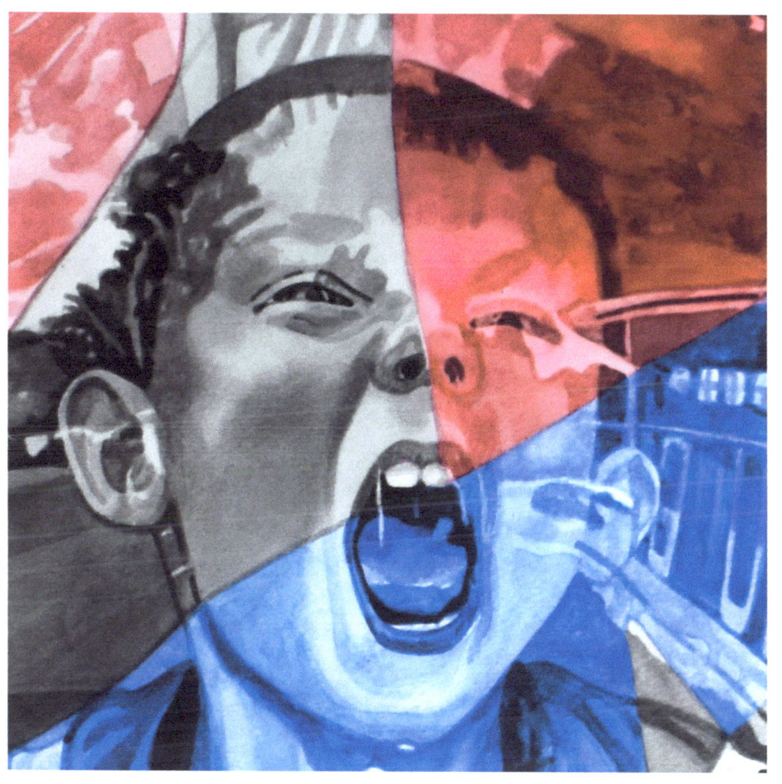

VISCERAL

Images have power. They can instantly generate trauma or swiftly create a state of catharsis. Once I realized the tremendous voice that power gave me, I developed not only a passion but a strong sense of responsibility. Painting, for me, is a refined form of communication. It has been my experience, again and again, that a picture truly is worth a thousand words.

Have you ever had the common nightmare that you have unwittingly arrived at work only to realize that you are naked or in your pajamas? *Arrival* resulted from that line of thinking. For new arrivals, Gotham can be an exciting place of opportunity. It can also be a place of crime, anxiety and disquietude. If you have ever felt alone amongst a group of friends or acquaintances, excluded and hesitant, you may sympathize with this work. The naked figure stands alone, vulnerable and uncertain, while nevertheless courageously facing onward. Inner confidence will manifest.

I used myself as model for this work. In the early to mid 2000s, I did this frequently. The reasons I modeled for myself so often are obvious: I was immediately available, I work for free, I was willing to appear vulnerable, and I knew exactly what I wanted in a pose.

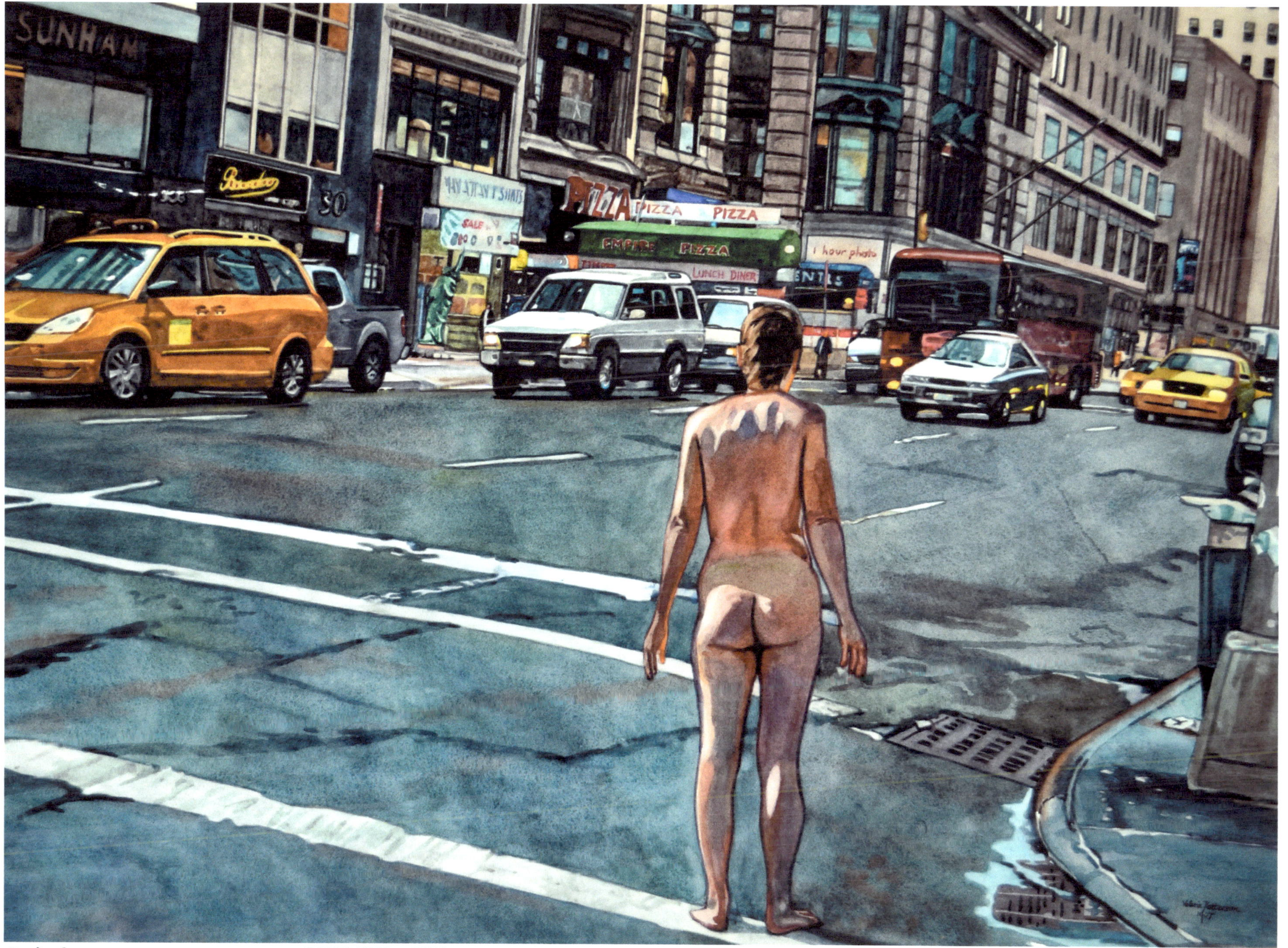

Arrival   2007 (27" x 35")

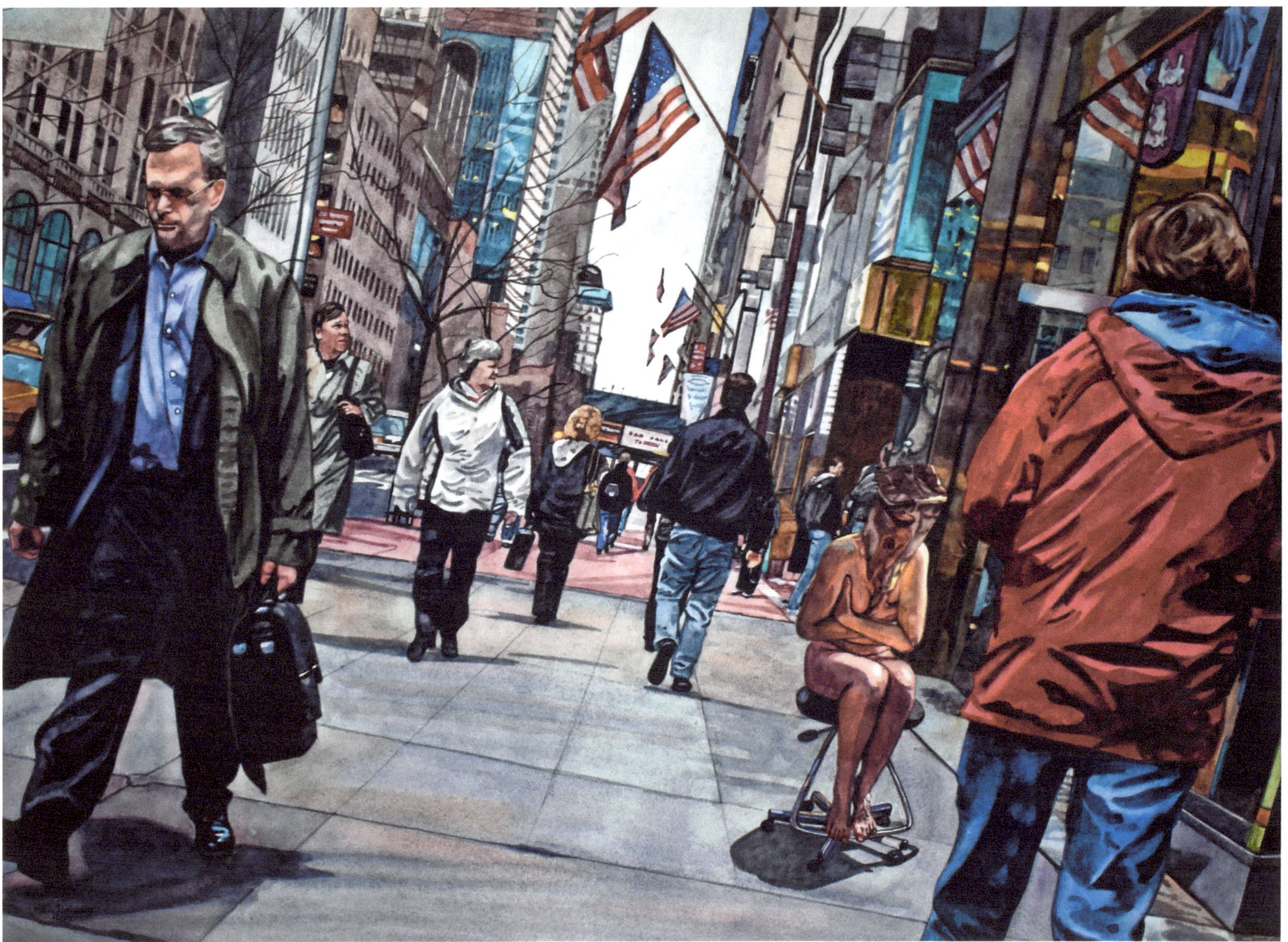

Ghost In The Machine   2007 (27" x 35")

Simply put, "ghost in the machine" means the consciousness, or mind, carried in a physical entity; the mind being a separate entity from the physical brain. This painting is a demonstration of what it can feel like to be overwhelmed and controlled by the mind, to allow anxiety and fear to dominate. While the naked, vulnerable, hooded person is suffering, no one else notices. She, and she alone, has created her reality and suffering.

Ghost In The Machine was a reopening of *Arrival*. They were created sequentially. It also expands upon my painting *Encompassed*. Once more, this work was done referencing two photos that just seemed to dance together on my studio floor.

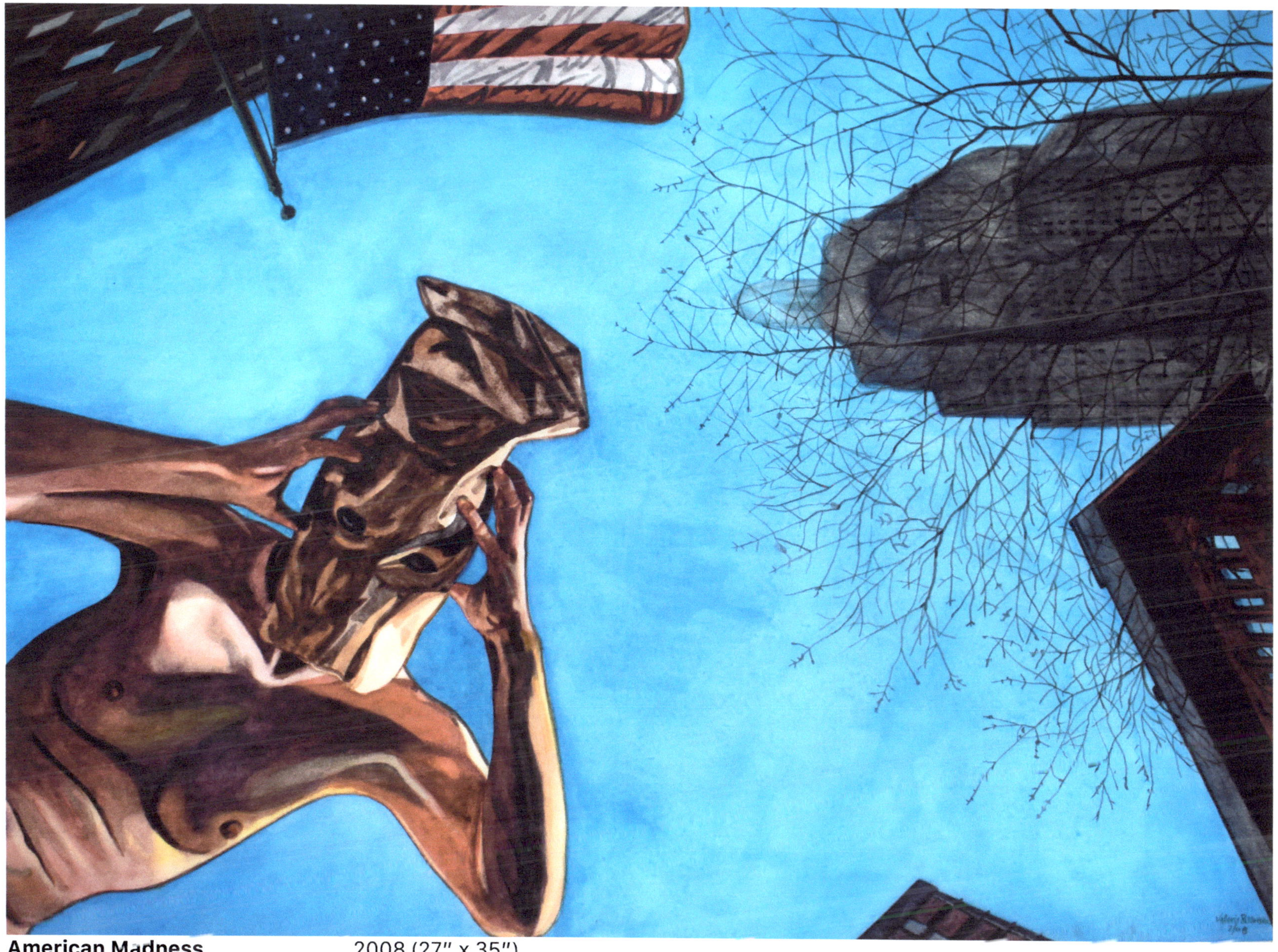

American Madness   2008 (27" x 35")

Political is personal and vice versa. Our political views are related to our identity, our sense of who we are in this dimension. Because of this, politics trigger our emotions. This painting reveals the lunacy that can result. I utilized two of my photos to create this image: one from NYC and another from a photo shoot of myself sporting a paper bag. The bag provides anonymity and symbolizes the bearing of much emotional weight. Representations of me wearing the bag also appear in the paintings *Woman Is The Other* and *Ghost In The Machine*. Created in 2008, this painting's relevance continues to endure.

This painting developed shortly after listening to a radio interview of a feminist writer (I don't recall her name) on NPR. She stated that in our society, man is The One. Therefore, by default, woman is The Other. The implications here were clear. If you are not The One then you are less worthy of dignity and respect. Members of The Other are "othered" by The One. Women often lack equality in status, rights and opportunities. We repeatedly feel anonymous, used, and in the shadows of The One. Yet, there is great strength that can develop from being "othered"; resilience and enlightenment commonly originate from adversity.

In this painting, I chose to illustrate how it feels to be The Other: faceless, naked and in a dark place. Nevertheless, the woman sits up straight and faces the viewer head on. The background was fashioned from a photograph of an Eastern State Penitentiary prison cell while the woman was constructed from a self-portrait photo.

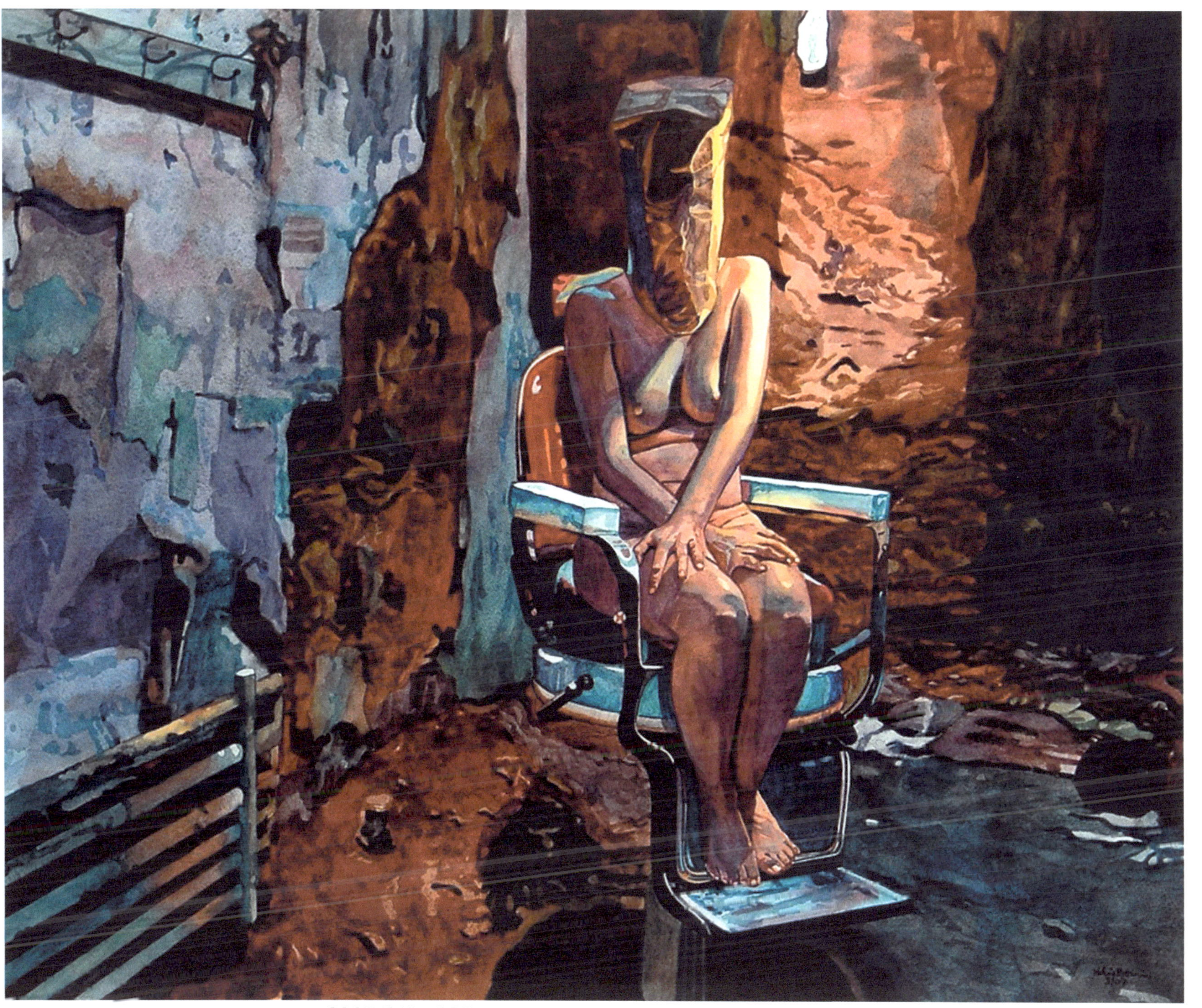

Woman Is The Other 2007 (31″ x 36″)

I recall several instances, as a child, hearing about people falling through the ice on the St. Lawrence River. In each instance the person was unable to be saved, and perished. I remember experiencing a powerful emotional response in the pit of my stomach while listening to the adult conversations concerning these events.

Decades later, I again felt this way while listening to the Kate Bush (English singer/songwriter) work *Under Ice. Under Ice*, on the surface, is a song about a dream a woman is having in which she falls through the ice while skating.

During the winter of 2004, I felt compelled to create a painting illustrating this. For a reference, I photographed myself (hands) behind my ice covered garage window. This generated a series: two paintings behind ice. Then, one night a while later, I awoke with the idea of a related spin off series. (See *Underneath*.)

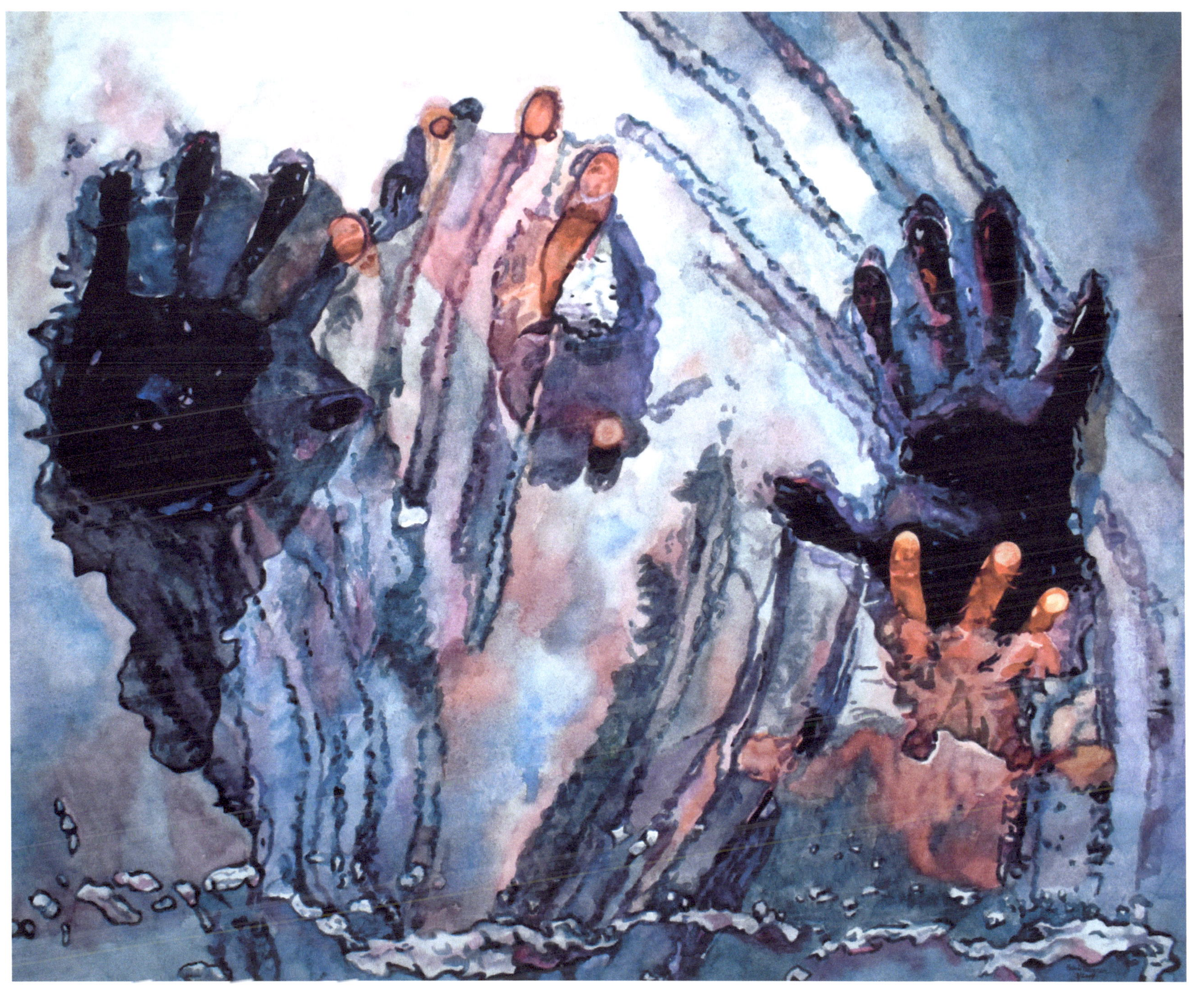

Under Ice   2004 (31″ x 36″)

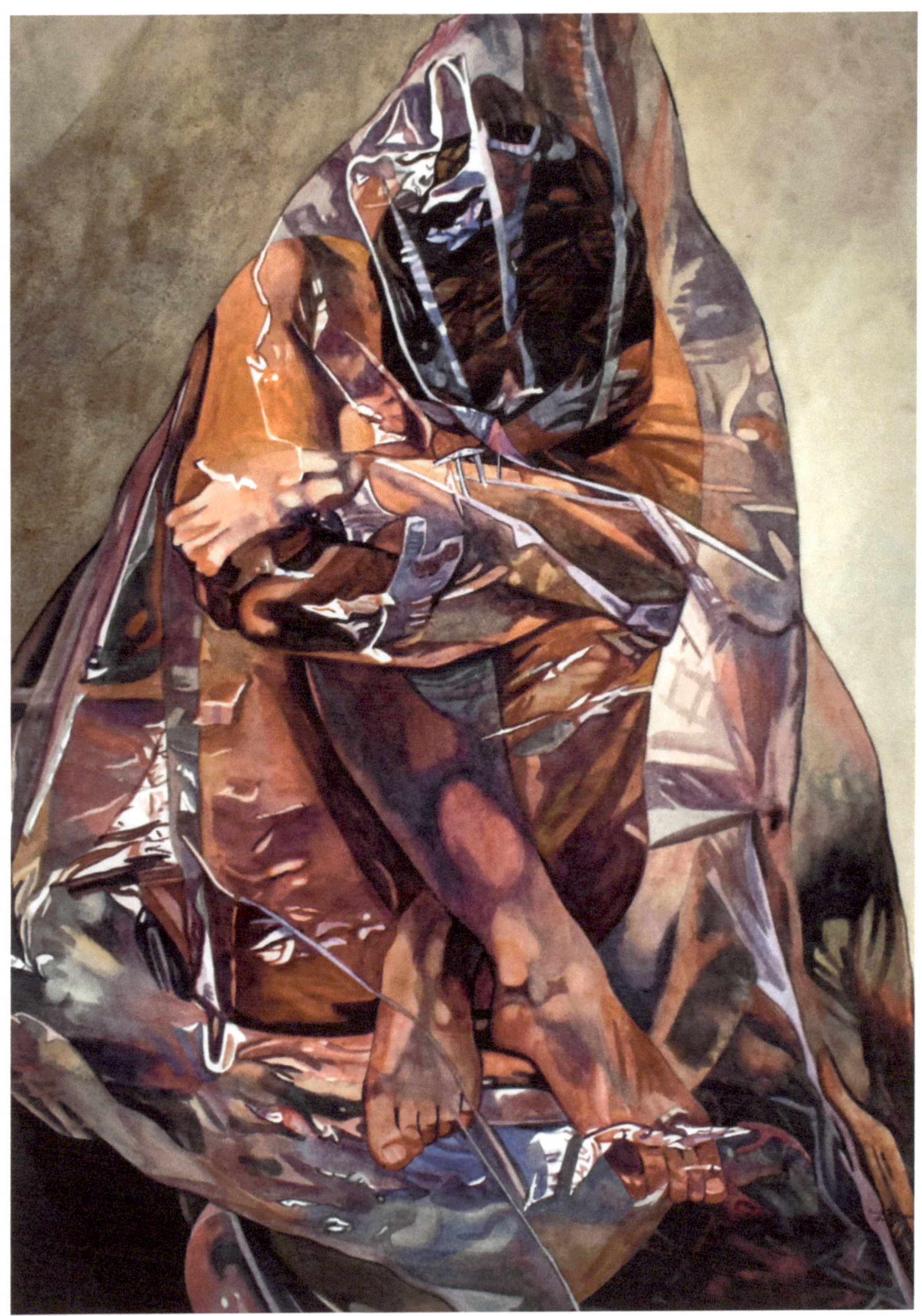

This painting illustrates how all encompassing it can feel when our thoughts and anxieties take over our minds. The nude, curled-up figure is vulnerable, yet secured within plastic wrapping. There is no escape as incessant musings torment.

The idea for this painting was born while contemplating the fate of a large plastic bag (which began its usefulness wrapped around a new appliance) that was hanging out on one of my kitchen chairs. I set my camera to auto, removed my clothes, put on the bag and voilà, reference photo!

Best to remember that thoughts are just thoughts, nothing more, nothing less.

Encompassed　　　　　2004 (39" x 30")

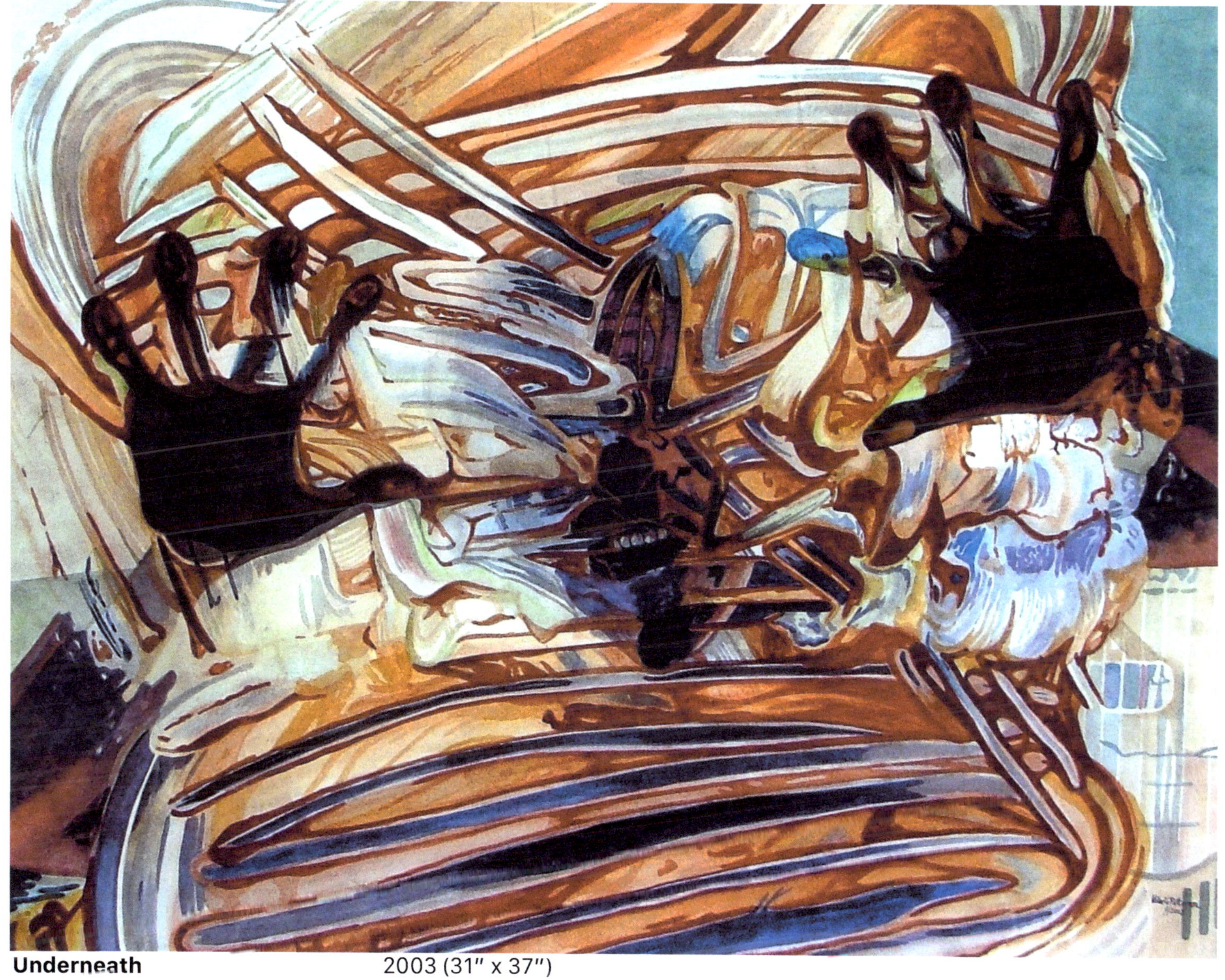

Underneath   2003 (31" x 37")

While working on *Under Ice*, I began considering what lies beneath the public facade that we each generate and maintain for the world to see. There are always emotions and thoughts we feel the need to conceal from others: those that we believe others will deem unacceptable in some way. Nonetheless, these truths and sentiments tend to announce themselves from time to time.

To create the photographs I worked from for this series, I combined ketchup and peanut butter (to symbolize a kind of primordial ooze), smeared it around on an inside window between my porch and living room, then photographed myself, through the glass, interacting with it. As previously mentioned, multiple paintings developed from the photos taken that day.

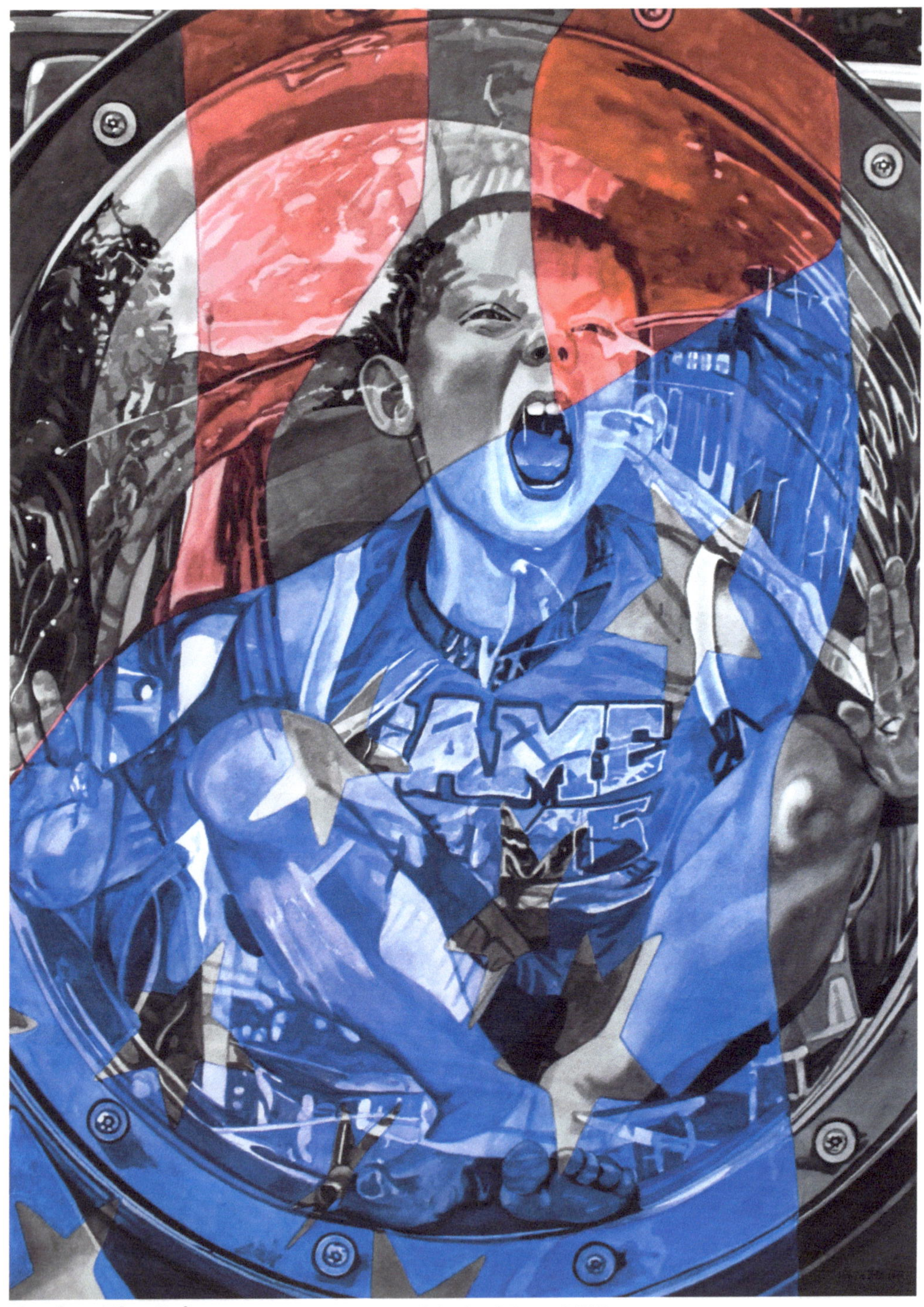

Politics, if you are paying attention, and even if you aren't, are affecting you. Decisions that we all must abide by, live with, and sometimes suffer through, are made for us every day by officials we elect — assuming we live within a democratic system. When politicians create policies that shame, divide or treat us inhumanely, the costs are incalculable. We break down when our physical and emotional needs can not be met.

This painting is an attempt to illustrate this kind of reaction and suffering. To this end, I commandeered a photo that I took of a family member play acting at a local playground; drew it in pencil; then painted in red, white and blue.

Paying The Price 2019 (35" x 27")

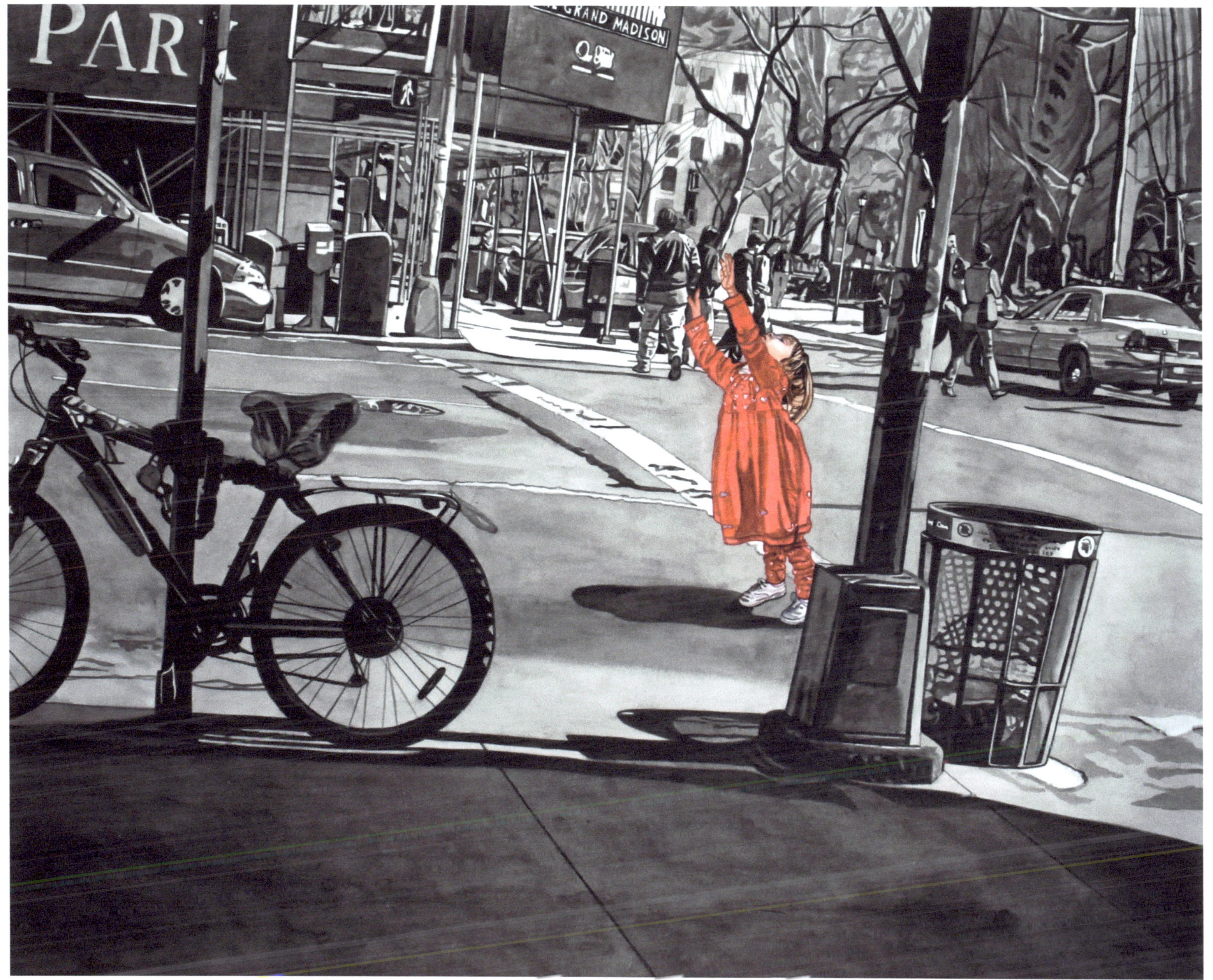

Response   2006 (30" x 37")

I don't specifically recall what prompted this work, but I do know that sometimes the world can be too much to bear. I expect that I was feeling under pressure at the time this idea/image manifested itself. We all long for help in the form of a higher power from time to time. Thus, the child reaches for assistance within the limits of the colorless NYC street. I believe that she will discover exactly what she cries out for.

This painting was created shortly after, and as the result of, the events of September 11, 2001. Most of us that lived through this period of time in the United States recall having been deeply disturbed and forever altered by the events of that day. I remember hearing about, and closely following, the horrific events on the radio that I had tuned to NPR while preparing for the day in my elementary-school art room. Disbelief and numbness followed for months afterwards.

When I saw images of this anonymous business man statue, entitled *Double Check* (by John Seward Johnson II), I began contemplating what survives disaster. John F. Kennedy once said, "Children are the world's most valuable resource and its best hope for the future." I agree. We, as a species, desperately need the innocence, purity, kindness, goodwill and love so often profoundly expressed by children — to survive and to rebuild.

The child in this painting survives in company with the work of art. Art is often considered the repository of a society's collective memory. How appropriate.

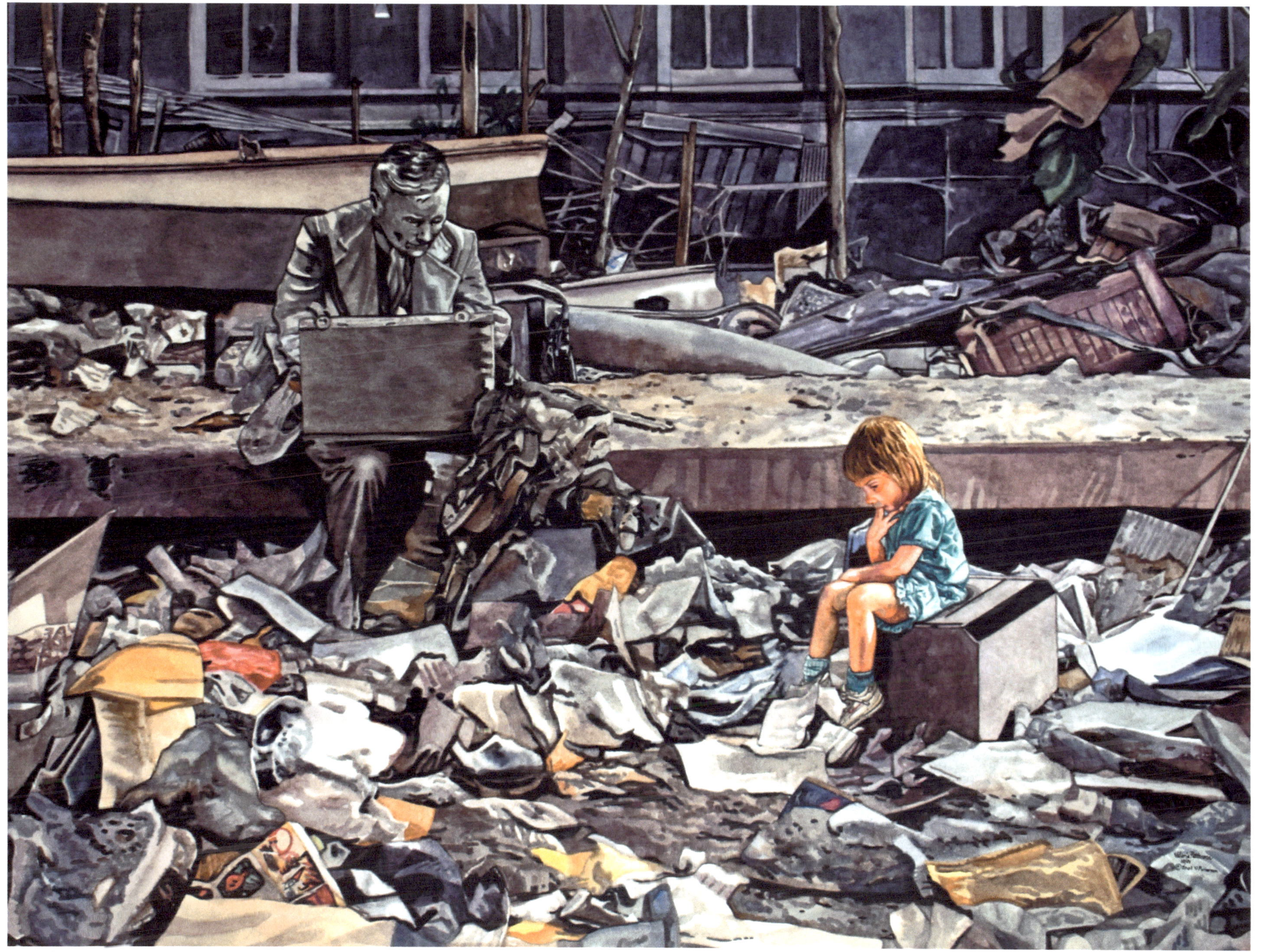

Survivors   2001 (27" x 34")

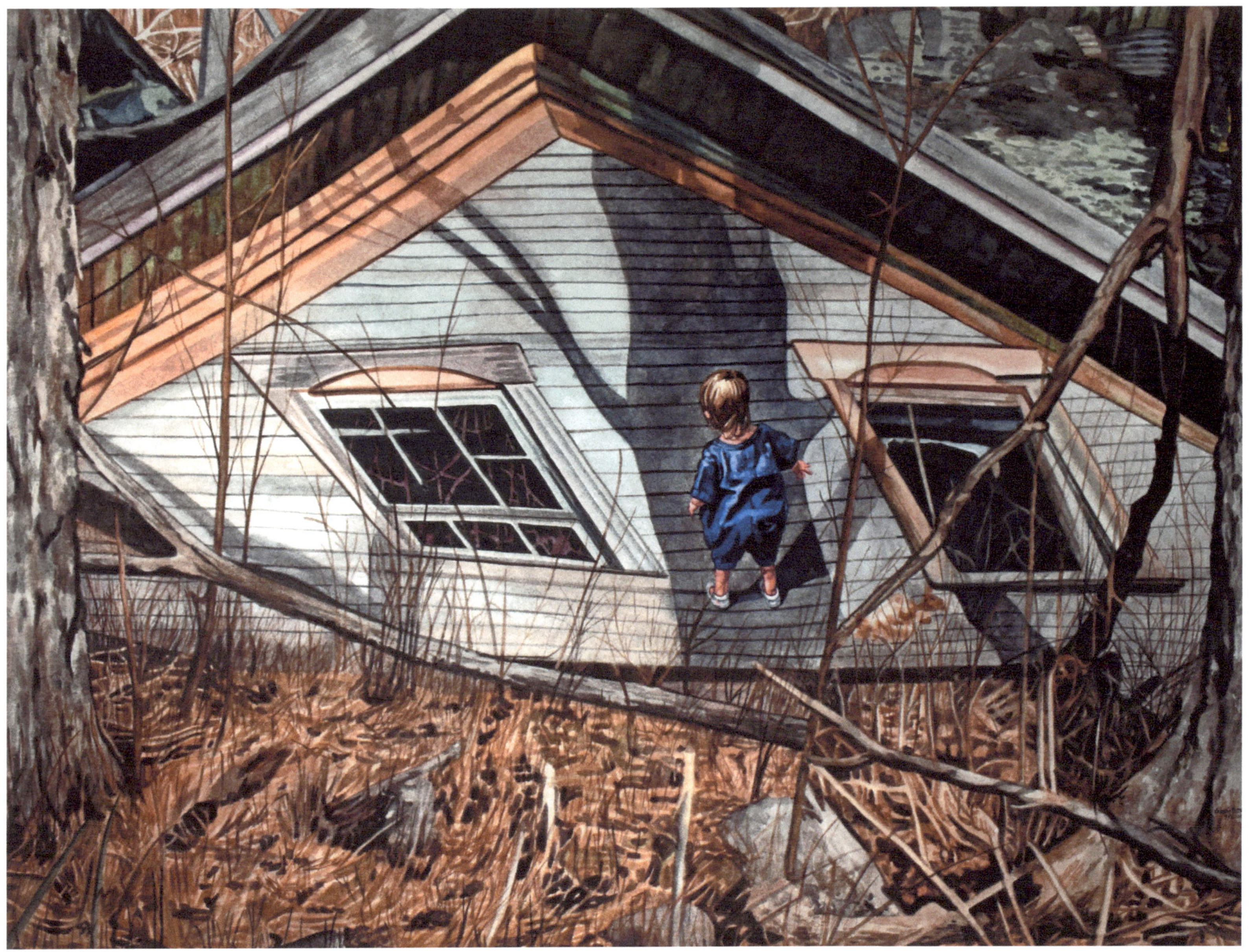

Collapsed   2001 (27" x 34")

The dilapidated house in this painting is one that resided down a side road near where I once lived. It captivated me. I wondered why someone, a property owner, would abandon it and sanction such deterioration. Over time, this house began to symbolize an extraordinary resilience. For years, it refused to completely topple. I added the young child walking up its wall (in my original photo, she was actually walking up the bottom of a playground slide). While on its surface this painting may appear rather ominous, for me it represents inner strength, courage and renewal.

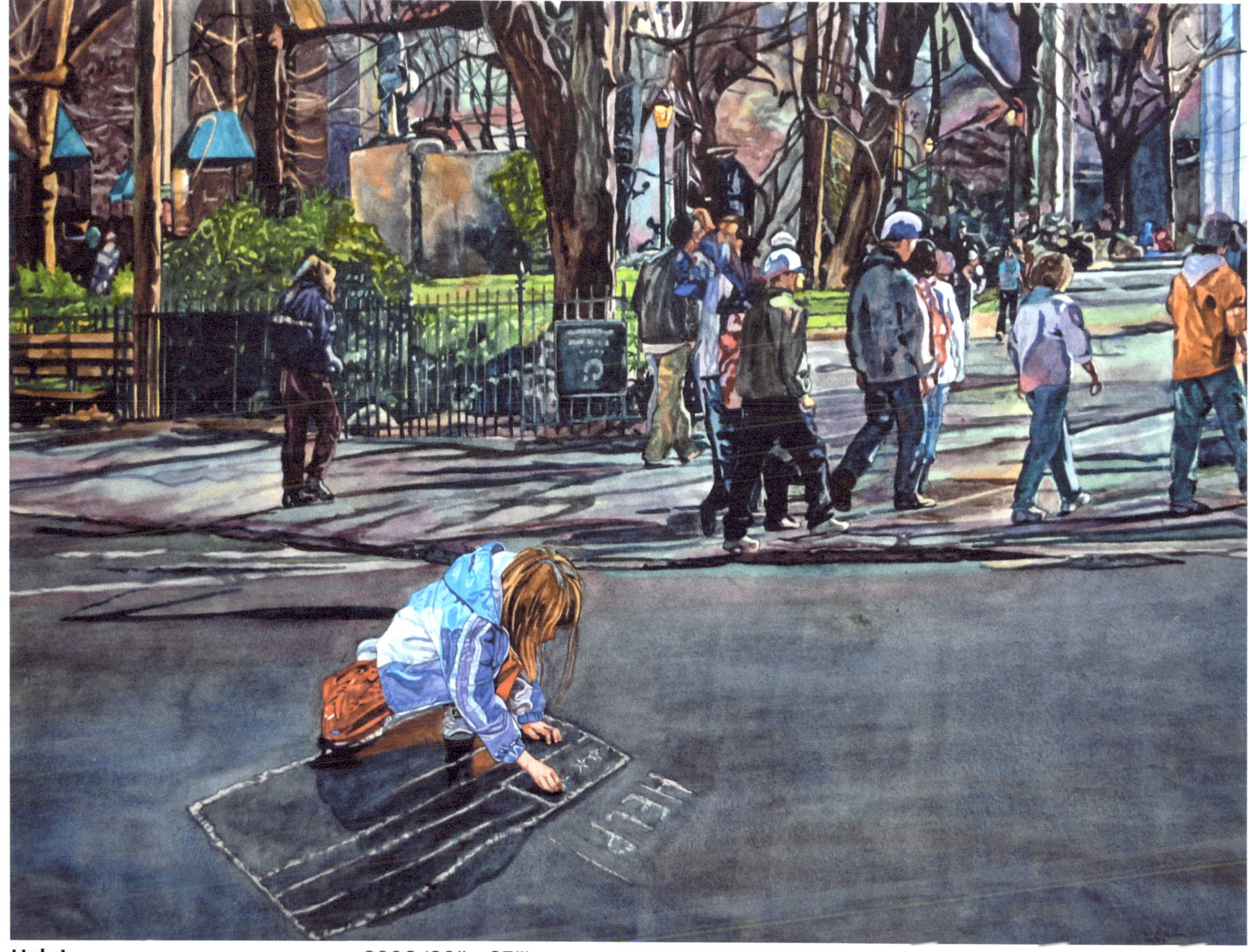

Help!   2006 (30" x 37")

As previously mentioned, I often scatter photos across the studio floor and see which ones join or merge together in some significant way. Once again that was the case with this painting. The first thing that I noticed was that all of the people in the cityscape photo that I took in NYC are looking and walking away from, and to the right of, the viewer. In another of my photos, I spotted the young girl contentedly drawing on her home's driveway. Immediately, in my mind's eye, I saw the two images together, added the word "help" (It appeared to spontaneously pop into my head – a frequent occurrence), tapped into some of the current political discord, and created this political work of art.

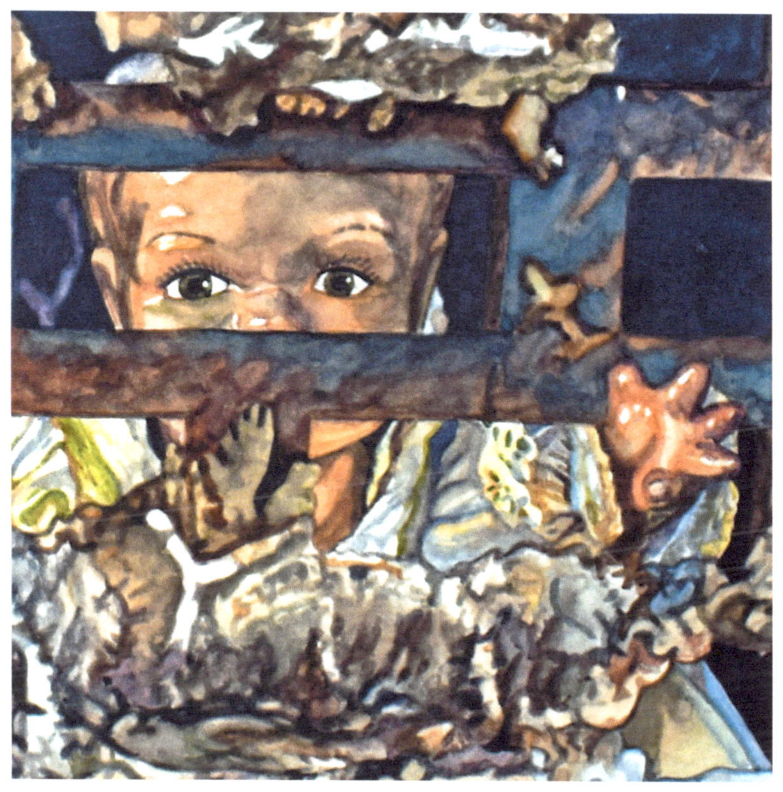

DISCOVERY

We acquire knowledge through experiences that alter and form us. The more we learn, the more our souls develop, understand and expand. Revelations are significant. The world has teeth and can inflict pain, but attitude can alter pain's meaning and intensity.

It took me too long to figure out just how crucial attitude is in this life. But I've got it now! The way we see and respond to events, situations and people shapes our everyday story. The energy that you put out really does come back to you. If you wake up on the wrong side of bed, so to speak, your entire day tends to follow suit. On the other hand, if you sustain optimistic thoughts and feelings about what exists and is transpiring around you, life proceeds accordingly. Some folks have a truly amazing ability to maintain a positive attitude even in the most challenging of situations. In this painting, a young girl does just that. As evidence, she draws a happy face on the floor of the deteriorating cell she is occupying. She has hope.

The cell in this artwork was created from a photograph taken at the Eastern State Penitentiary in Philadelphia, PA. The young lady was painted from a photo of a family member drawing outside.

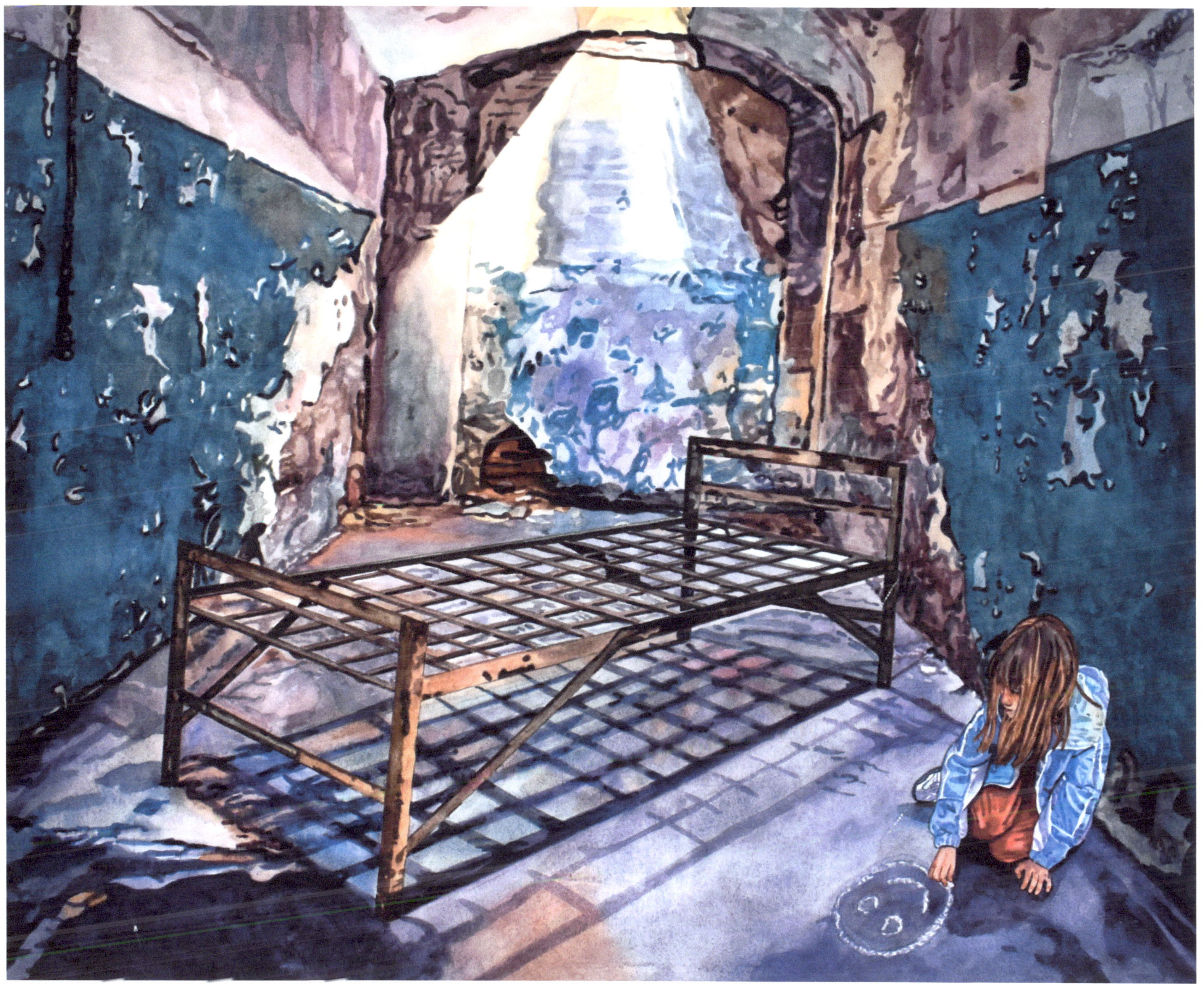

Attitude 2006 (31″ x 37″)

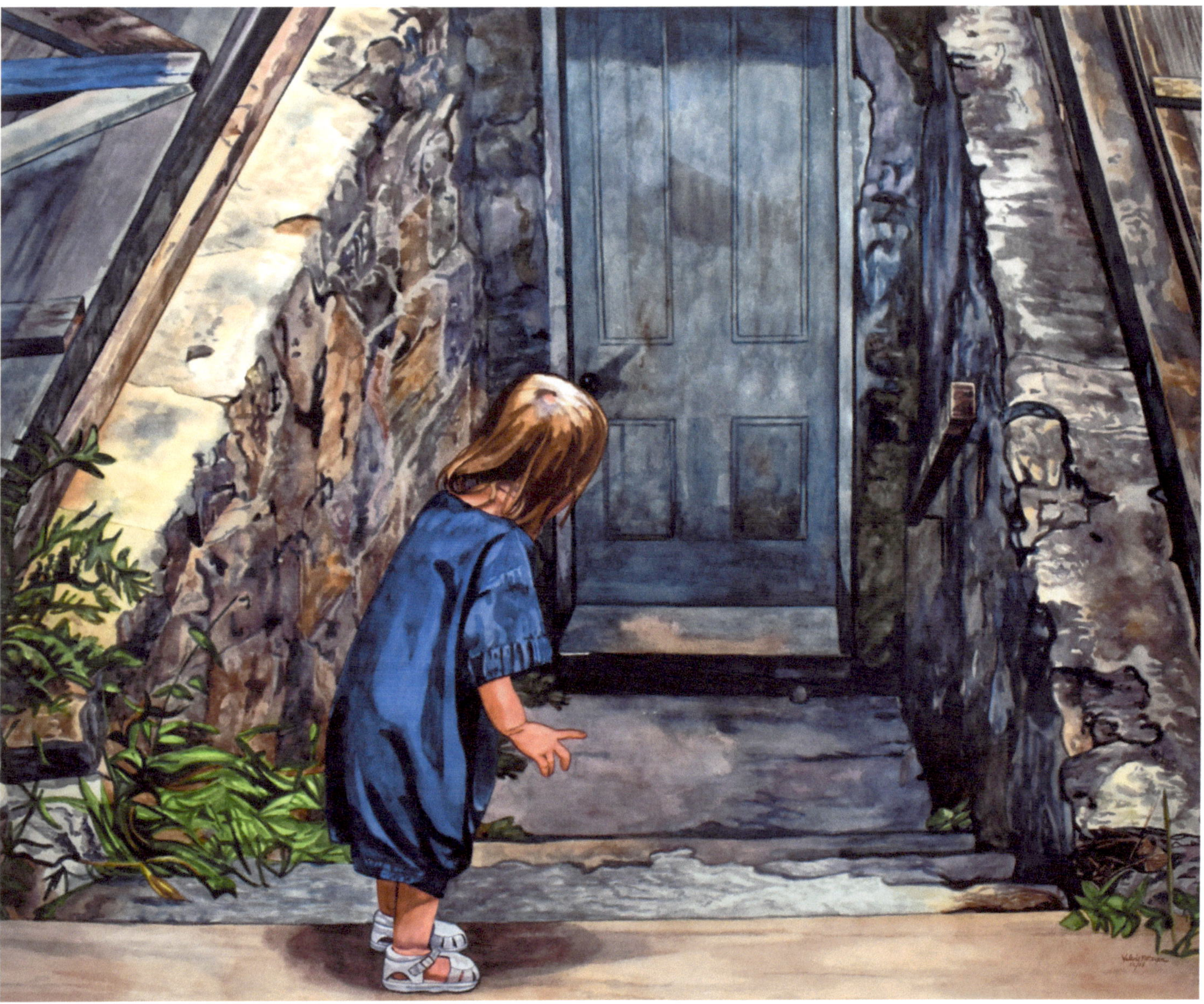

Curiosity   2005 (31″ x 37″)

We arrive into this world possessing an ebullient spirit of inquiry. This interest and wonder is most important to our intellectual and psychological development. Curiosity encourages us to question, imagine and ponder. Conversely, It is sometimes responsible for introducing us into hazardous circumstances: learning experiences, if you will. I have always found outdoor basement entrances alluring and a little scary. I am curious about where, and to what, they lead. As well, they represent a possible breach of security. Here, an innocent, inquisitive, child peers down a set of outdoor basement steps. What will she encounter? The staircase may suggest a passage. Will she descend the stairs? If so, what will she discover there? What will happen next? Will there be enlightenment? If so, will it be beneficial or unfavorable?

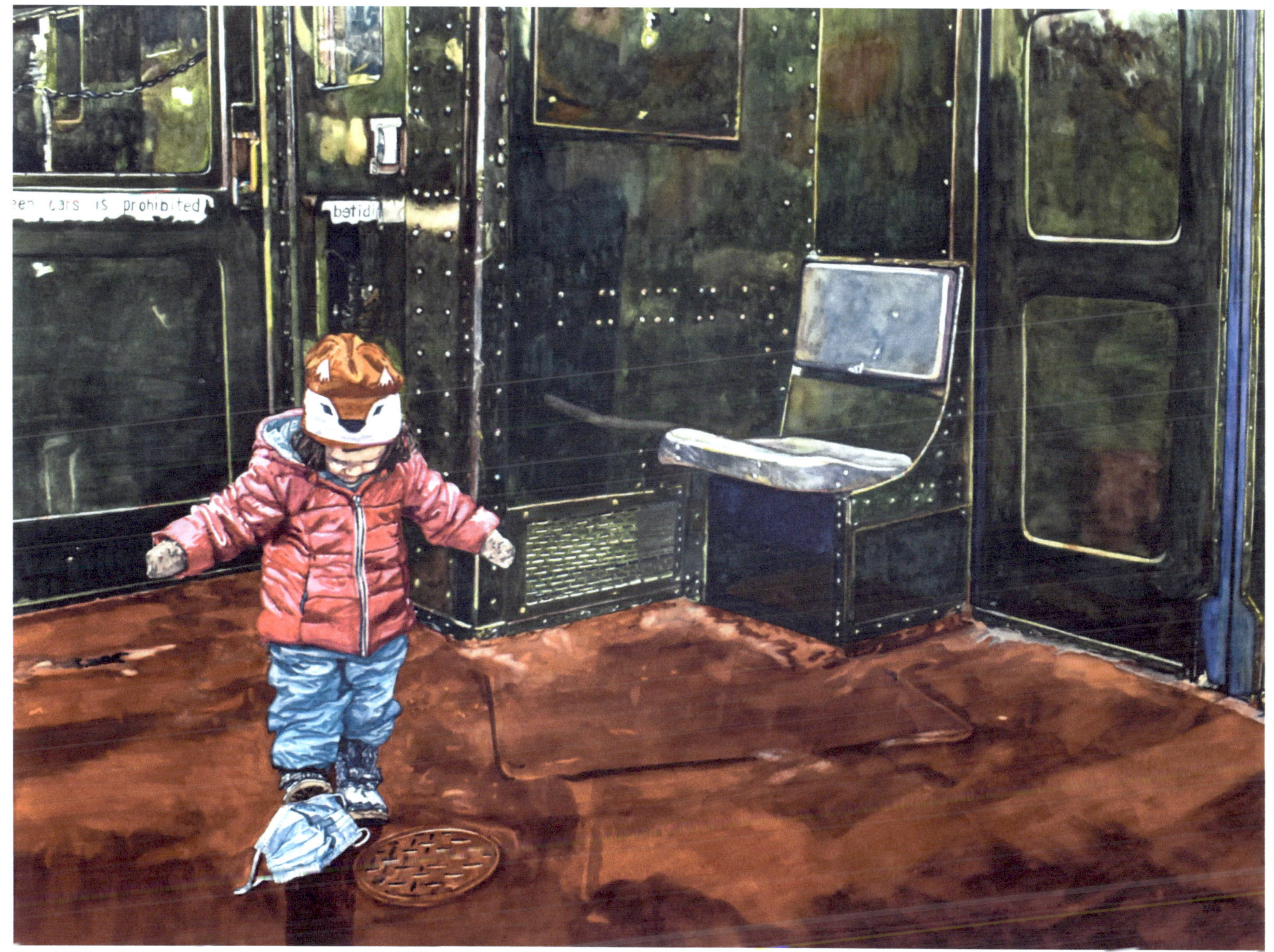

Prohibited Prerequisite   2022 (27" x 35")

Covid-19 mask mandates and their retractions have been so numerous, during the pandemic, as to cause the average person apoplexy. Mask wearing recommendations from the World Health Organization, the CDC and state governors have changed so often that many have stopped following altogether. While I have been an ardent mask wearer from the start, believing that we all need to take care of ourselves and each other, even I have begun paying less attention. As Covid infections endure, I simply assume wearing a mask is more preferable than not wearing one. This image is the result of the frustration that I have felt over all of this indecision and uncertainty. The child, my own inner child perhaps, rails against her mask (the disease), kicking it across the floor of the subway train. Yet, she remains alone and in peril as the disease rages on.

When I paint, I nearly always listen to audiobooks. When I heard this quote, I wrote it down straight away for future reference. There was unquestionably a painting in it. It is the world's bite that devours our innocence and sense of well-being. I no longer recall when the world first bit me, but I do remember many subsequent bites. One that I continue to carry with me occurred at the age of six. My best friend decided that the new girl in the neighborhood was more fun than I was. So, the two of them shunned me. I ran home crying. My Mother, hearing my sobs, met me on our front porch. She asked me where I was hurt. At that time, I was only acquainted with physical pain, especially as a cause for crying; so, I said that I wasn't hurt. Questioning me further, my mother discovered what had happened with my best friend. Then and there she defined and described emotional pain to me, explaining that it can often be worse than physical pain.

How right she was.

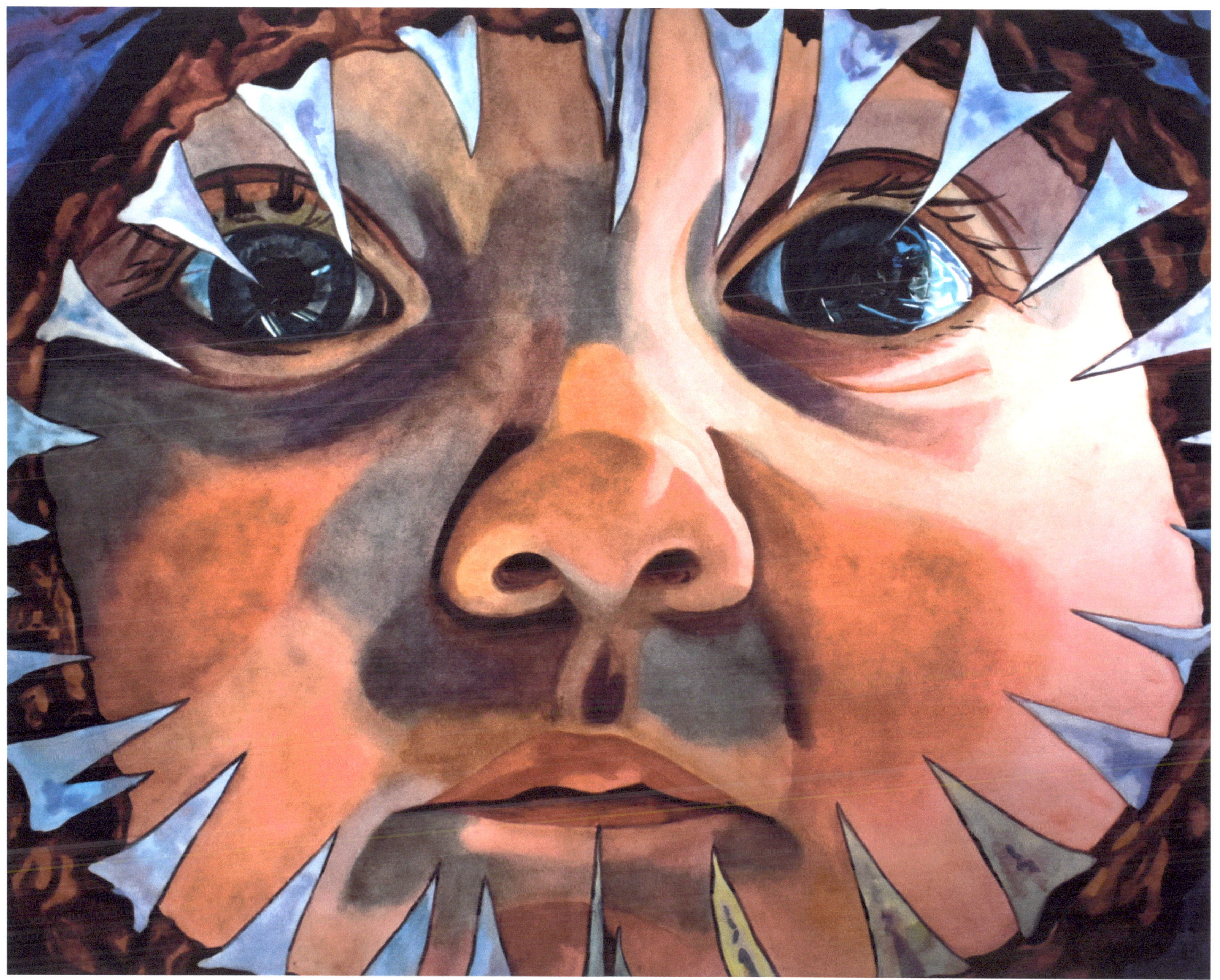

The World Has Teeth   2006 (31" x 37")

I have been a huge Beatles fan since childhood. I own nearly every album that they released, on both vinyl and CD. I have spent many hours listening to their music, from childhood to the present. So, while in New York City during 2007, visiting Central Park's Strawberry Fields was a must. On that day, there were many flowers lovingly placed around the monument in the shape of a peace sign. It was powerful, and I instantly knew that I had to paint it. Weeks later, while contemplating this photo, I again felt an urge to incorporate a young child with her clarity and purpose. Among my boxes of photos, I discovered just the right image of this young member of my clan riding her big wheel. Free from guilt or blame, she rides across the monument's surface glancing back and setting the importance of peace in her mind and life. I changed the proportion of the child (making her very small compared to the actual size of the monument) for dramatic effect.

Viewing this painting today, years after its completion, I continue to wonder how we presume that we can keep our children safe and secure when we refuse peace? Most of us teach our children to focus on building friendship, trust and collaborative relationships, so when and how does that get lost? When do, and did, we become so disoriented?

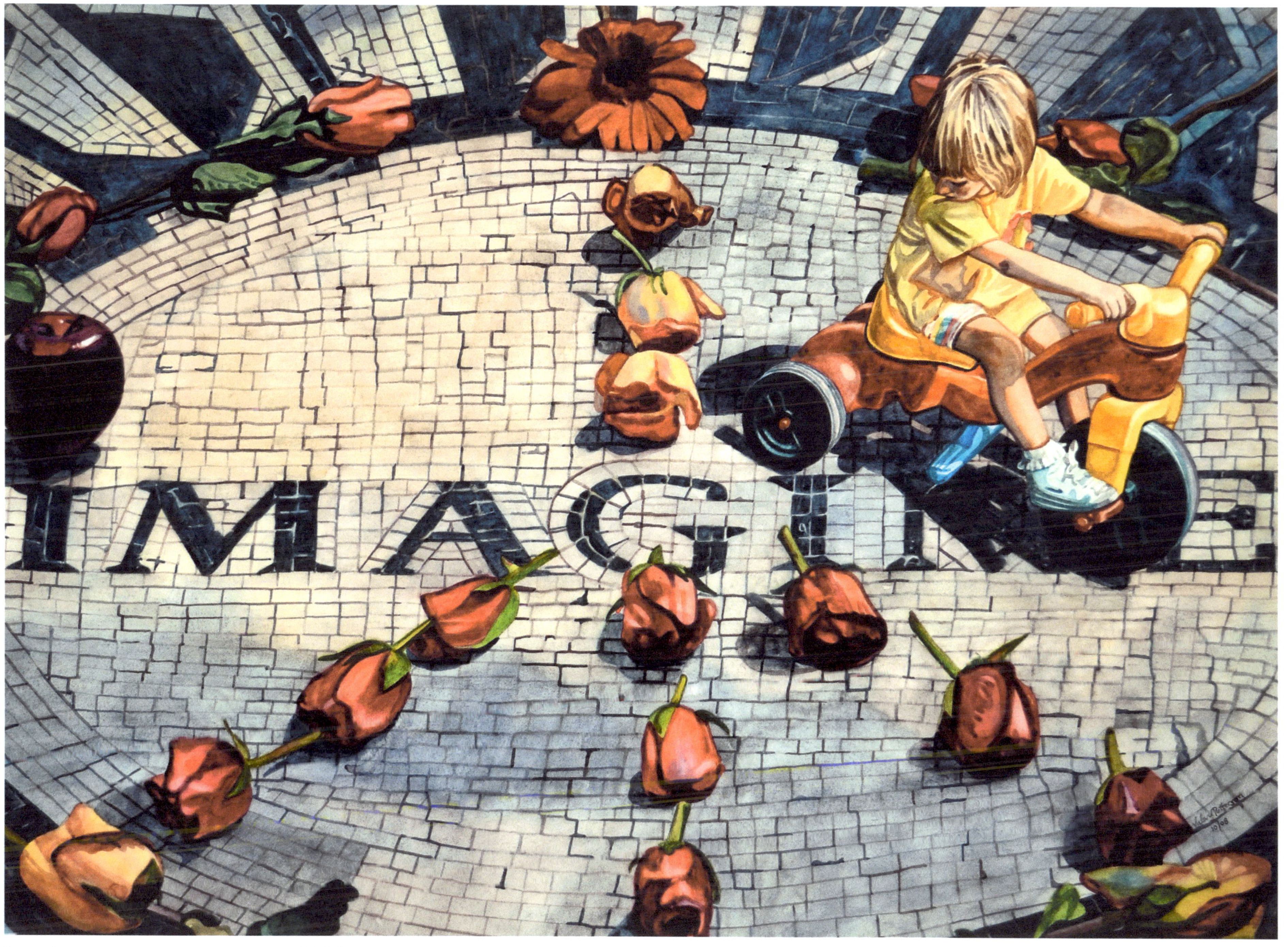

Imagine   2008 (27" x 35")

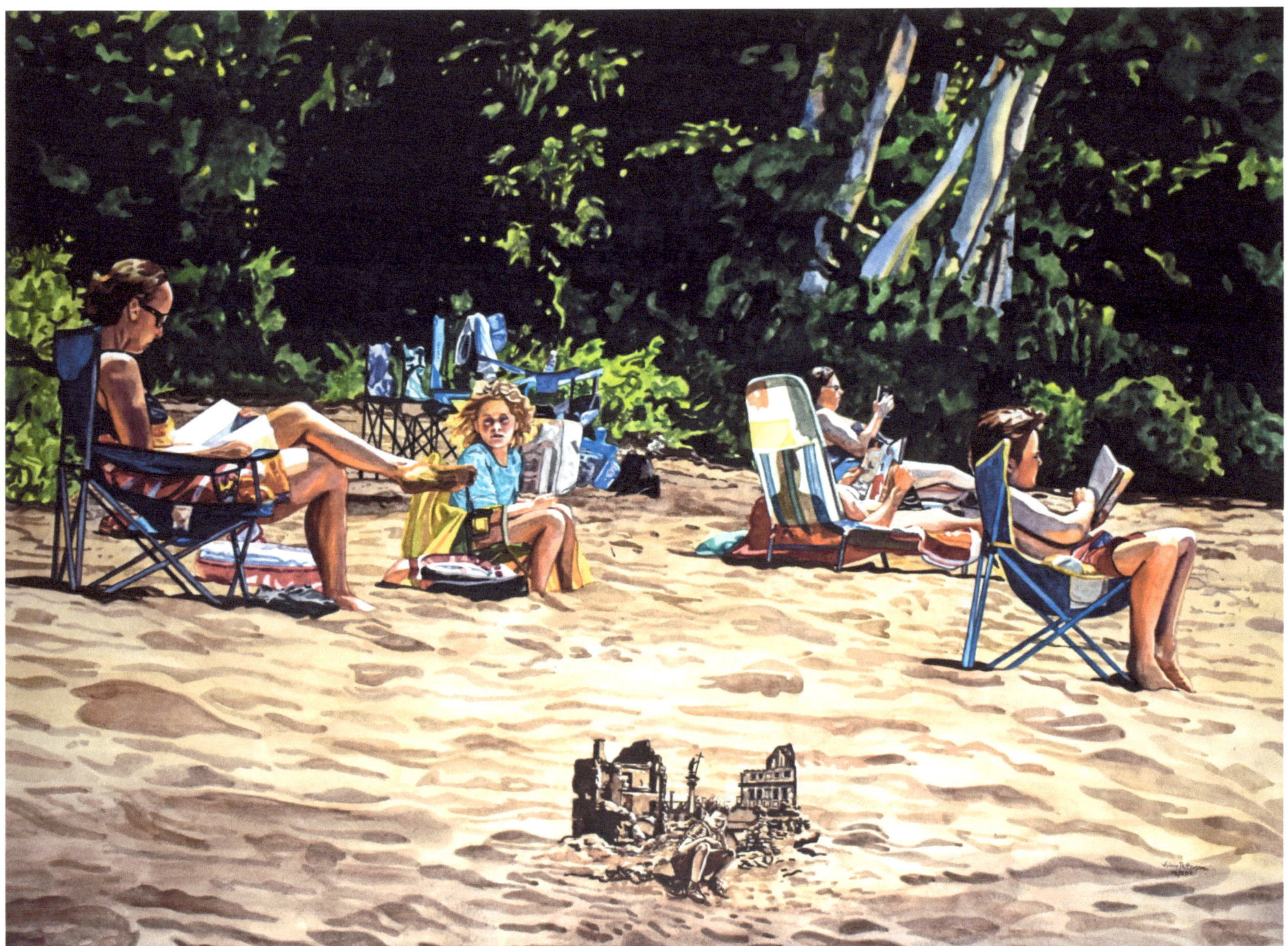

Great Read   2001 (27" x 35")

I randomly shot the photograph used for the main part of this work one morning at Lake Clear beach, one of my favorite Adirondack summer haunts. Weeks later, viewing the photo while contemplating a new idea for a painting, I noticed that all of the people, except one, are reading. The young girl near the center was somewhat wistfully looking out towards me. My mind began to wander. I wondered what all of those people were reading; and what would happen if what they were reading were to manifest on the beach? Perhaps they would all be so engrossed in their literature that they wouldn't notice — except for one very intuitive, observant, adolescent girl. In my mind's eye, a fragment of World War II history revealed itself in the sand. A teenage boy was included within the ruins, perhaps drawing the attention of the girl glancing his way.

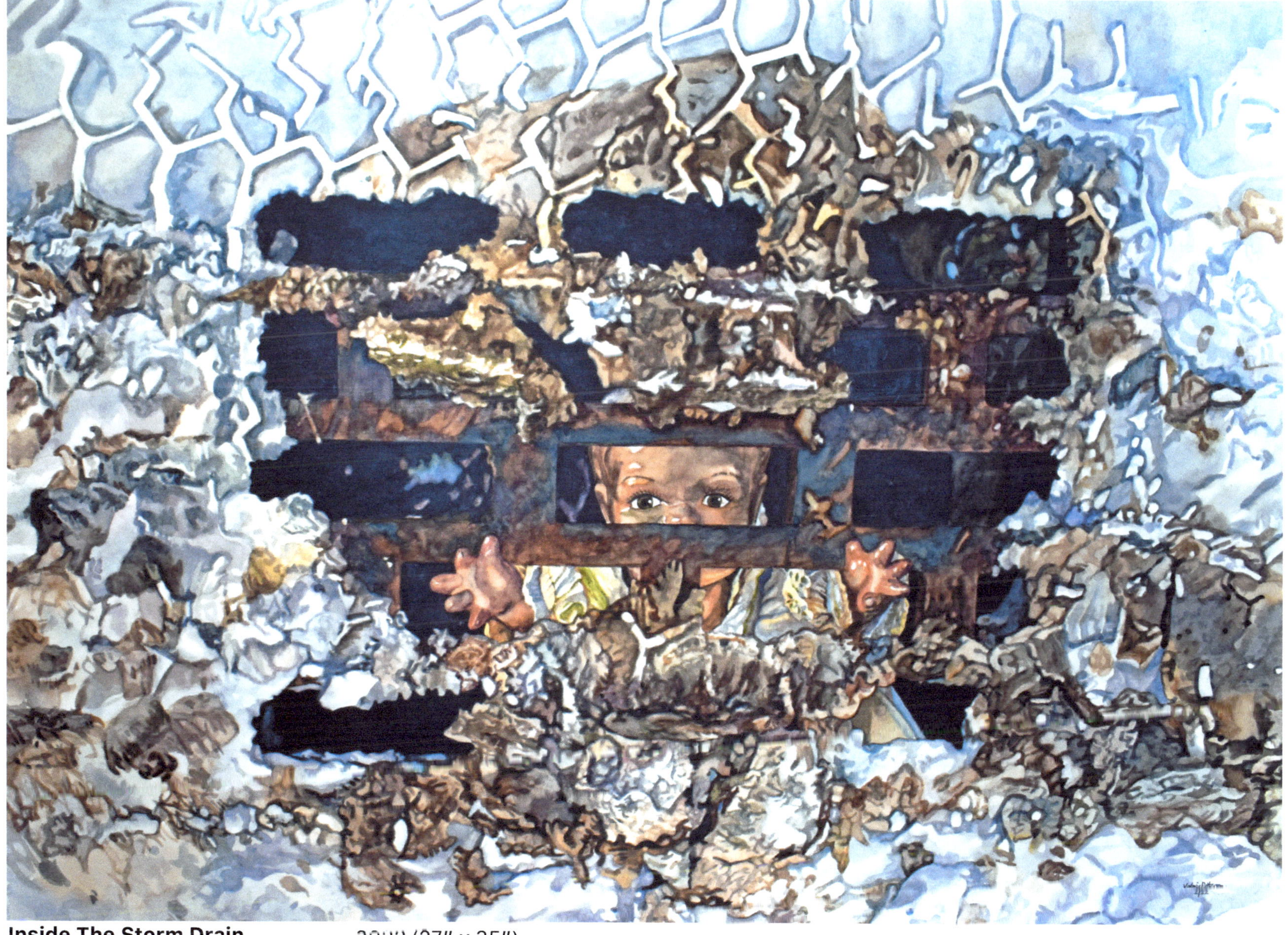

Inside The Storm Drain   2022 (27" x 35")

This storm drain exists at the end of the street I live on. Passing it on a winter walk, I found it visually captivating and photographed it. I knew forthwith that, if I painted it, something atypical would have to emanate from the dark hollow behind the grate. The photo was around for several years when, one afternoon in my studio, I glanced over at Kathleen Marie (the antique doll). It was her little almost cartoonish hands that first grabbed my attention. In my mind's eye, I saw this tiny hand emerging from behind my sewer grate. That was it! Yes, I am a Stephen King fan. And, yes, *It* is one of his works that I treasure. So, perhaps this painting is an homage of sorts.

In 2008 I visited the Susan B. Anthony House Museum in Rochester, NY. Near the museum, off West Main Street, is the Susan B. Anthony Park where this sculpture of Ms. Anthony and Frederick Douglass resides (*Let's Have Tea* by Pepsy M. Kettavong). Ms. Anthony was one of the most visible leaders of the women's suffrage movement; a champion of temperance, abolition and equal pay for equal work. Visiting her former home and learning more about her humanitarianism, fortitude and accomplishments was tremendously inspiring to me. Grievously, as is the case with much of women's history in the United States, her accomplishments are given little more than a modest mention within most public-education curricula. I certainly never learned about her in school. What a revelation it was for me, discovering some of the amazing achievements of Ms. Anthony and many other women!

This painting illustrates the moment that a young girl discovers a piece of her story. Knowing the history (or **her**story, in this case) of one's gender opens up an awareness of what is possible, builds respect and fosters self esteem. It is paramount.

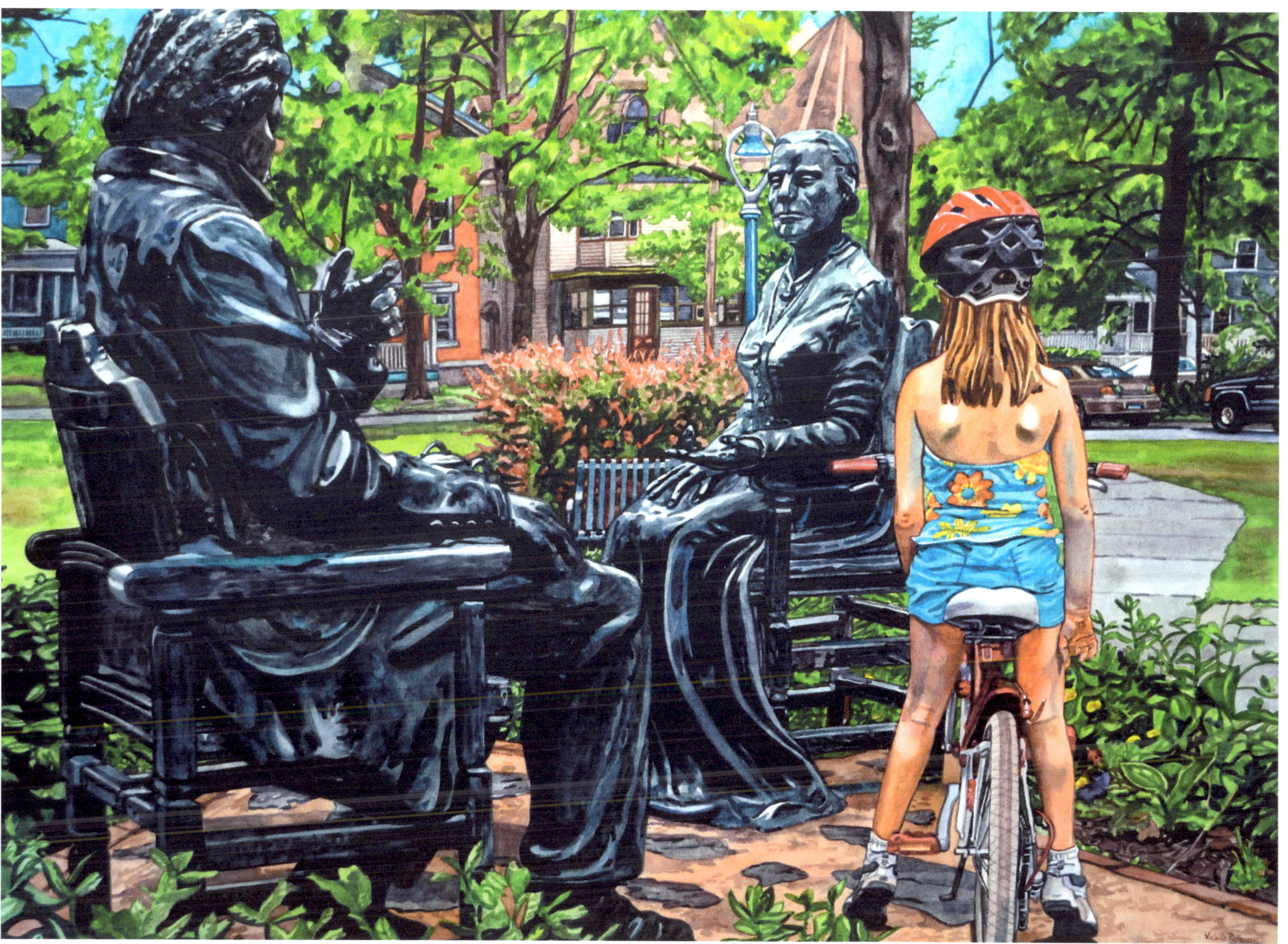

Discovering Susan B. Anthony   2008 (27" x 35")

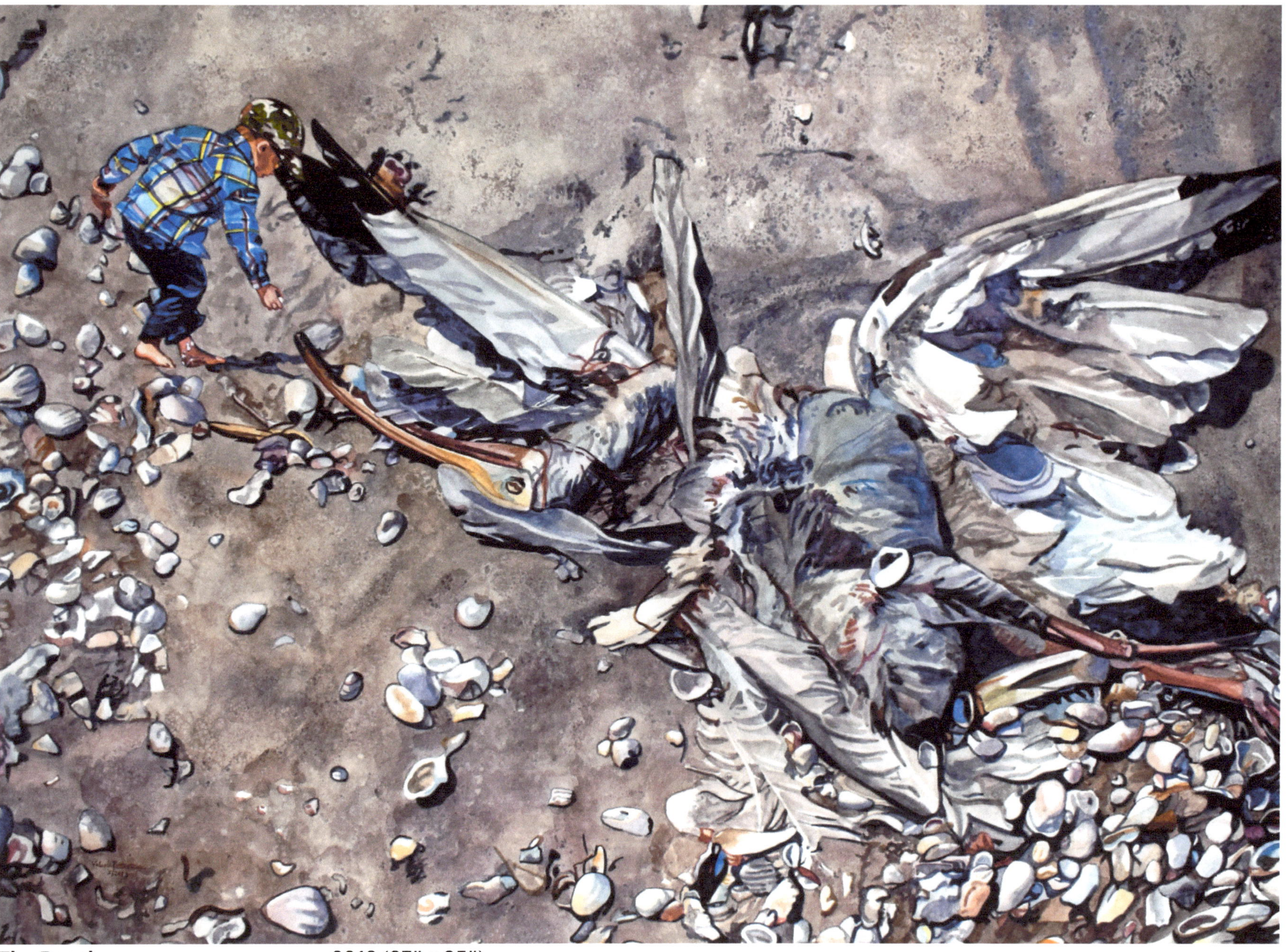

The Beach   2013 (27" x 35")

I came across the remains of this bird while visiting a Sanibel Island beach. Further down the shoreline, I observed the young boy. For me, the two together create a moment of discovery, an uncovering and learning. How effortlessly and suddenly death can intrude on a typical afternoon. Yet, life intrudes too in the embodiment of youth.

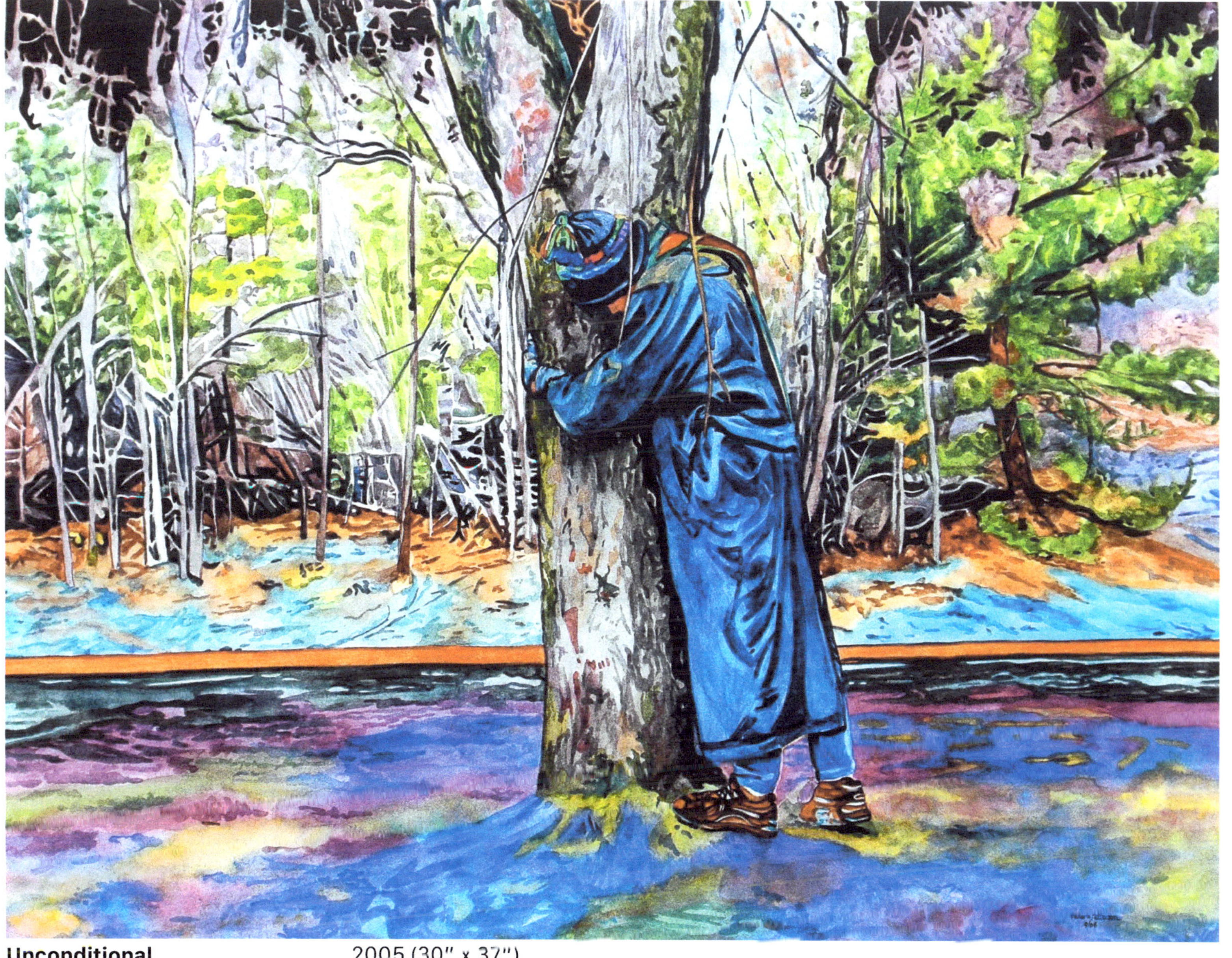

Unconditional 2005 (30" x 37")

Love without strings attached. Affections without any limitations. Try as we may, we humans have clearly not mastered this notion. Some of nature has though. Connecting with nature has been proven to be good for our mental and physical health. Hug a tree when no one else is around. It works for me. Try it, I dare you! The figure here (Me, dressed up — I staged this scene) is reflexively hiding, well concealed within a long coat and hat symbolizing a loss of emotional well being. The tree (from my former front yard) provides the necessary unconditional love. I used vibrant, somewhat psychedelic, colors to disclose the magic transpiring.

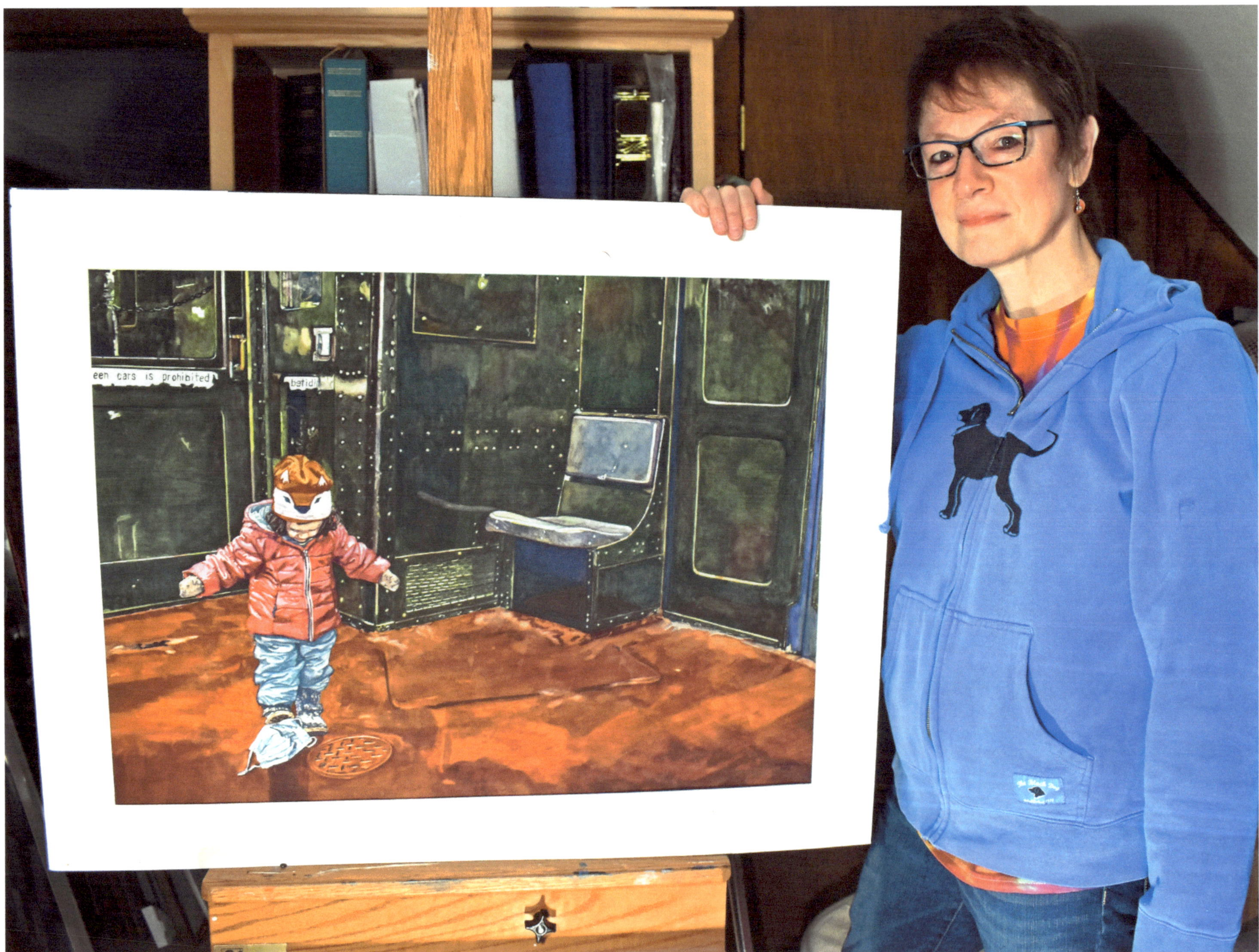

een cars is prohibited

About the Artist

Born in 1963, Patterson grew up in Ogdensburg, NY, the daughter of a Presbyterian Minister and public school teacher whom she credits for her humanitarianism.

An excruciatingly shy child, Patterson spent much of her time alone: thinking, feeling, dreaming and watching... Her interest in art began in earnest in Junior High School, when she quickly learned that she could communicate more easily visually.

Patterson earned degrees in both art and education, followed by careers spanning nearly 40 years creating and teaching art.

Asked when she decided to focus on art that conveys social and political messages, Patterson responded, "It gradually evolved as I was creating art that was meaningful to me. Once I realized the tremendous power that images can have to make people comfortable or uncomfortable, happy or sad, settled or unsettled, I knew I had a voice. I decided to use my voice to encourage people to see, think and feel — something not always valued in our culture."

Patterson's award-winning watercolor paintings have been exhibited extensively throughout the United States in both group and solo exhibitions. These include The Bond St. Gallery in Brooklyn, NY; The Torpedo Factory Art Center in Alexandria, VA; The Arts & Literature Laboratory in New Haven CT; The Frederic Remington Art Museum in Ogdensburg, NY; The Baltimore Watercolor Society in Baltimore, MD; The Schweinfurth Art Center in Auburn, NY; The Visual Arts Center At Clarington, Ontario, Canada; The Fredericksburg Center For Creative Arts in Fredericksburg, VA; and Lake Placid Center For The Arts in Lake Placid, NY.

Patterson's awards include: First Prize in The Dayton Ohio International Peace Museum, Art for Peace International Juried Exhibition. Juror's Award Of Excellence for the Annmarie Sculpture Garden and Arts Center, National Juried Exhibition: "Ebb & Flow: The Power Of Water." Several Awards of Excellence and a Featured Artist Award from Manhattan Arts International. And, the Nelda Howell Memorial Award from the Hudson Valley Art Association's 72nd Annual National Juried Art Exhibition (Hastings-On-Hudson, NY).

Index of Paintings

www.ingramcontent.com/pod-product-compliance
Lightning Source LLC
Chambersburg PA
CBHW042032050726

47599CB00006B/875